STEP-BY-STEP GUIDE TO CORRECT ENGLISH

BY MARY ANN SPENCER PULASKI, Ph. D.

ARCO PUBLISHING, INC.
NEW YORK

TO CHARLIE

Without whose help this book
would never have been written

Published by Arco Publishing, Inc.
215 Park Avenue South, New York, N.Y. 10003

Library of Congress Cataloging in Publication Data

Pulaski, Mary Ann Spencer.
Step-by-step guide to correct English.

Revision of: 1974 ed.
1. English language—Composition and exercises—Programmed instruction. 2. English language—Grammar—1950- —Programmed instruction.
I. Title.
PE1409.5.P84 1981 420'.7'7 81-4657
ISBN 0-668-05277-5 AACR2

Printed in the United States of America

Contents

Introduction

This book is designed for people who want to learn how to write correctly in English. To do this, you must learn the basic parts of a sentence. You must also learn how to put these parts together to make a good sentence. Words are the building blocks of language. This book will help you understand how to arrange your words clearly and correctly. Then you will be able to communicate with others, and they will understand and remember what you say.

Many different people—the Greeks, the Romans, the Anglo-Saxons, and the French—have influenced the development of the English language. For this reason, English may seem difficult at times. However, it will become easier as you learn how to use words to construct good, clear sentences.

This book is carefully constructed to help you discover where you need to begin your study. First it provides a diagnostic test that covers most of the material presented in the book. Answer as many questions as you can; then turn to the answer key at the end of the test and correct your work. This will help you evaluate your particular strengths and weaknesses.

The diagnostic test is divided into several sections. Each section has a heading such as *Nouns* or *Adverbs*. Wherever you make mistakes you should study the exercises covering that material. Look in the Table of Contents to find the chapters you need to study. If you make no errors in a section, skip those exercises and go on to the material that gives you trouble. You may need to study only the more advanced exercises, or perhaps only certain areas such as punctuation. Taking this test will save you time and help you study more efficiently.

You will find that this book begins with the very simplest two-word sentences and gradually builds up to much longer compound sentences. All the kinds of words we use—nouns, verbs, adjectives, adverbs, etc.—are explained and used in exercises of increasing difficulty. At the back of the book is an answer key so that you can correct your errors after each exercise and perform better on the next one. There are many exercises in punctuation and capitalization, as well as model letters for writing to a friend or to a business. Reviews are frequent, and a long final test helps you make sure that you really understand how to use simple English in its proper form. Handy tear-out pages are provided so that you can easily remove individual exercises from the book.

If you use this book correctly, you will find at the end that you are no longer making the mistakes you did on the diagnostic test at the beginning. This is because you now understand the structure of sentences and the function of the words that go into them.

The ability to use language correctly is a very powerful tool. The purpose of this book is to help you write and speak better, so that you, too, will be able to communicate effectively with the world around you.

Diagnostic Test

Take this test to find out how much you know about using English and what you need to study to improve your skills. Use the answer key that follows this test to check your answers.

I. **Subjects:** Draw a line under the subjects in each of the following sentences.

1. The boy yelled.
2. Dark threatening clouds gathered overhead.
3. Joe and Tony played catch.
4. I went to the grocery store.
5. In the dark sky shone the bright stars.
6. An eagle soared over the lake.
7. Chicago is in Illinois.
8. Julie washed the dishes and Betsy dried them.

Answer the following:

1. Why does *an* (and not *a*) come before *eagle* in sentence 6?

   ____

2. Each subject in the above sentences (except in sentence 4) is the name of a person, place, or thing. What is the grammatical term for such a word?

   ____

3. What is the grammatical term for the word "I" in sentence 4? ____________

4. In sentence 2, find the simple subject and write it here. ________________

5. Write the complete subject of sentence 2 here. ________________________

   ____

6. Find a compound subject in one of the preceding sentences and write it here.

   ____

7. Find the subjects of a compound sentence and write them here. ____________

   ____

II. **Predicates:** Draw a vertical line separating the subject from the predicate in each of the following sentences. Write S above the subject and P above the predicate.

1. Birds fly.
2. The team played hard.
3. The crowd shouted and cheered.
4. Maria is the oldest woman in the office.
5. Overhead roared a jet plane.

6. The day was bright and sunny.
7. In the distance we heard the band.
8. Charlie threw Jim a fast ball.
9. I am the best pitcher on the team.
10. The boys fought and kicked the intruder.

III. **Nouns:** Answer the following.

1. Draw a line under every noun in the sentences above. How many did you find? ________
2. Find an example of a common noun in sentence 6. ________

   ____
3. Find proper nouns in sentences 4 and 8.

   ____
4. Find a plural noun. ________
5. Find a singular noun in sentence 9.

   ____
6. Find a collective noun in sentence 3.

   ____
7. Find a predicate noun in sentence 4.

   ____
8. Find the noun that is the direct object in sentence 10. ________
9. Find a noun that is the indirect object in sentence 8. ________
10. Write the plural or singular form of the following nouns.

wolf	________
story	________
radio	________
key	________
hero	________
________	wives
________	mice
________	oxen
________	teeth
________	sheep

IV. **Verbs:** Find the verbs in the following sentences and draw two lines under them.

1. The caged lion roared fiercely.
2. It is a beautiful day.
3. High in the treetop the bird sings.
4. We were late to work.
5. All night long the baby cried.

Answer the following using the examples above:

1. Give an example of a verb expressing action in the past. ________

   ____
2. Give an example of a verb expressing action in the present. ________

3. Give an example of a verb expressing being in the past.

____

4. Give an example of a verb expressing being in the present.

____

5. Give the present or past tense of the following irregular verbs.

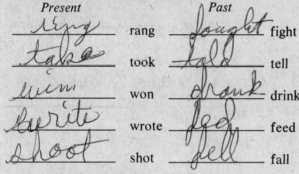

Present		*Past*	
________	rang	________	fight
________	took	________	tell
________	won	________	drink
________	wrote	________	feed
________	shot	________	fall

V. **Pronouns:** Underline all the pronouns in the following sentences.

1. She went to the movies with me.
2. We took them to the ball game.
3. He and I are good friends with them.
4. You can come with us to visit him.
5. They put her on the stretcher.

In the sentences above, some pronouns are used as subjects and some are used as objects. List them below according to how they are used.

SUBJECTS	OBJECTS
________	________
________	________
________	________
________	________
________	________
________	________

VI. **Adjectives:** Circle all the adjectives in the following sentences and draw an arrow to the words they describe.

1. The fat little boy ran down the dusty street.
2. That tall blond girl is the smartest in the whole senior class.
3. She certainly is intelligent!

Answer the following:

1. In the above sentences find an adjective in the predicate that describes the subject. ______________
2. Give the comparative forms of the adjective "little." ______________
____
3. Give the comparative forms of "intelligent." ______________
____

VII. **Adverbs:** Circle all the adverbs in the following sentences. Draw an arrow to the words they modify.

1. Slowly and painfully he hobbled up the mountain.

2. The beautifully decorated room was very impressive to me.

3. Very quietly he walked down the steps.

Answer the following:

1. For each adverb above ending in "ly," write below the adjective from which it was formed.

______________ ______________

______________ ______________

2. Is "good" an adjective or an adverb?

3. Is "too" an adjective or an adverb?

4. Is "there" an adjective or an adverb?

5. Is "their" an adjective or an adverb?

VIII. **Prepositions:** Find the prepositional phrases in the preceding sentences. List below each preposition and its object.

PREPOSITIONS	OBJECTS
______________	______________
______________	______________
______________	______________

IX. **Conjunctions and Interjections:** Circle the conjunctions and underline the interjections in the following sentences.

1. Oh, darn! I hooked it, but it got away!

2. Hey, wait for Tony and me.

3. Wow, did you see that?

4. I'm late because I got lost.

X. **Kinds of Sentences:** There are four kinds of sentences. You will find an example of each kind in the preceding exercise. Write the term that tells what kind of sentence it is.

Sentence 1 ________________________

Sentence 2 ________________________

Sentence 3 ________________________

Sentence 4 ________________________

Every sentence must express a complete thought. Draw a line through any incomplete sentences below. Separate run-on sentences by using the proper punctuation.

1. First he shined his shoes then he took a shower.

2. Opening the window and shouting at him.

3. He put a sinker on the line it sank into the water.

4. As soon as breakfast was over.

XI. **Punctuation and Capitalization:** Put capitals and punctuation in the following sentences as needed.

1. turn up the tv said her mother dont you want to hear the news

2. hank aaron broke babe ruths home run record in april 1974

3. <u>the</u> <u>daily</u> <u>news</u> is published at 220 e 42 st new york n y

4. gen eisenhower became president of the usa

5. dr john f sawyer has office hours from 9 am to 2 pm on mondays and fridays

6. oh dear i forgot to buy lettuce eggs and milk

7. mr tribuno my boss called me into the managers office
8. this was his order screws bolts nuts nails washers
9. its such a mess i cant stand it
10. the childrens toys and the boys bicycles are all over the yard
11. shouldnt the cat eat its dinner
12. john please pass the butter said his father
13. sir i admit your general rule
    that every poet is a fool
    but you yourself may serve to show it
    that every fool is not a poet
    Samuel Taylor Coleridge
14. hear me o lord when i cry unto thee
15. columbus discovered america on oct 12 1492

Answer Key for Diagnostic Test

I.

1. The boy yelled.
2. Dark threatening clouds gathered overhead.
3. Joe and Tony played catch.
4. I went to the grocery store.
5. In the dark sky shone the bright stars.
6. An eagle soared over the lake.
7. Chicago is in Illinois.
8. Julie washed the dishes and Betsy dried them.

1. Why does *an* (and not *a*) come before *eagle* in sentence 6? "An" is used before words that begin with a vowel.
2. Each subject in the above sentences (except in sentence 4) is the name of a person, place, or thing. What is the grammatical term for such a word? Noun.
3. What is the grammatical term for the word "I" in sentence 4? Pronoun
4. In sentence 2, find the simple subject and write it here. Clouds
5. Write the complete subject of sentence 2 here. Dark threatening clouds.
6. Find a compound subject in one of the preceding sentences and write it here. Joe and Tony
7. Find the subjects of a compound sentence and write them here. Julie, Betsy

II.

1. Birds (S) | fly (P).
2. The team (S) | played (P) hard.
3. The crowd (S) | shouted (P) and cheered.
4. Maria (S) | is (P) the oldest woman in the office.
5. Overhead roared (P) | a jet plane (S).
6. The day (S) | was (P) bright and sunny.
7. In the distance we (S) | heard (P) the band.
8. Charlie (S) | threw (P) Jim a fast ball.

9. I|am the best pitcher on the team.

10. The boys|fought and kicked the intruder.

III.

1. Draw a line under every noun in the sentences above. How many did you find? 17

2. Find an example of a common noun in sentence 6. day

3. Find proper nouns in sentences 4 and 8. Maria, Charlie, Jim.

4. Find a plural noun. birds, boys.

5. Find a singular noun in sentence 9. pitcher.

6. Find a collective noun in sentence 3. crowd.

7. Find a predicate noun in sentence 4. woman

8. Find the noun that is the direct object in sentence 10. intruder

9. Find a noun that is the indirect object in sentence 8. Jim

10. Write the plural or singular form of the following nouns.

wolf wolves

story stories

radio radios

key keys

hero heroes

wife wives

mouse mice

ox oxen

tooth teeth

sheep sheep

IV.

1. The caged lion roared fiercely.
2. It is a beautiful day.
3. High in the treetop the bird sings.
4. We were late to work.
5. All night long the baby cried.

1. Give an example of a verb expressing action in the past. roared, cried.

2. Give an example of a verb expressing action in the present. sings.

3. Give an example of a verb expressing being in the past. were.

4. Give an example of a verb expressing being in the present. is.

5. Give the present or past tense of the following irregular verbs.

ring	fought
take	told
win	drank
write	fed
shoot	fell

V.

1. She went to the movies with me.
2. We took them to the ball game.
3. He and I are good friends with them.
4. You can come with us to visit him.
5. They put her on the stretcher.

SUBJECTS	OBJECTS
She	me
We	them
He	us
I	him
You	her
They	

VI.

1. The fat little boy ran down the dusty street.
2. That tall blonde girl is the smartest in the whole senior class.
3. She certainly is intelligent!

1. In the above sentences find an adjective in the predicate that describes the subject. smartest, intelligent.
2. Give the comparative forms of the adjective "little." littler, littlest
3. Give the comparative forms of "intelligent." more intelligent, most intelligent

VII.

1. Slowly and painfully he hobbled up the mountain.
2. The beautifully decorated room was very impressive to me.
3. Very quietly he walked down the steps.

1.

slow	beautiful
painful	quiet

2. adjective
3. adverb
4. adverb
5. adjective

VIII.

PREPOSITIONS	OBJECTS
up	mountain
to	me
down	steps

IX.

1. Oh, darn! I hooked it, (but) it got away!
2. Hey, wait for Tony (and) me.
3. Wow, did you see that?
4. I'm late (because) I got lost.

X. Sentence 1 Exclamation

Sentence 2 Command

Sentence 3 Question

Sentence 4 Statement

Every sentence must express a complete thought. Draw a line through any incomplete sentences below. Separate run-on sentences by using the proper punctuation.

1. First he shined his shoes. Then he took a shower.
2. ~~Opening the window and shouting at him.~~
3. He put a sinker on the line. It sank into the water.
4. ~~As soon as breakfast was over.~~

XI.

1. "Turn up the TV," said her mother. "Don't you want to hear the news?"
2. Hank Aaron broke Babe Ruth's home run record in April, 1974.
3. The Daily News is published at 220 E. 42 St., New York, N.Y.
4. Gen. Eisenhower became president of the U.S.A.
5. Dr. John F. Sawyer has office hours from 9 A.M. to 2 P.M. on Mondays and Fridays.
6. Oh dear, I forgot to buy lettuce, eggs, and milk.
7. Mr. Tribuno, my boss, called me into the manager's office.
8. This was his order: screws, bolts, nuts, nails, washers.
9. It's such a mess I can't stand it!
10. The children's toys and the boys' bicycles are all over the yard.
11. Shouldn't the cat eat its dinner?
12. "John, please pass the butter," said his father.
13. Sir, I admit your general rule,
That every poet is a fool,
But you yourself may serve to show it,
That every fool is not a poet.

    Samuel Taylor Coleridge
14. Hear me, O Lord, when I cry unto Thee.
15. Columbus discovered America on Oct. 12, 1492.

Chapter 1

Subjects and Predicates

In English every sentence must have two parts: a *subject* and a *predicate*. The subject is the person or thing that performs some action; the predicate tells what the subject does.

Example

Dogs bark.

Here *dogs* is the subject which performs the action, and *bark* is the predicate, which tells what dogs do. Words such as *dogs, men, fish, table,* or *ball* are called *nouns*. They are the *names* of people, places, or things. Nouns are the subjects of all the sentences below.

The words that express the action in a sentence—what the subject does—are called *verbs*. The verb is the main word in the predicate. It is usually the easiest word to find. In separating a sentence into its subject and predicate, always LOOK FOR THE ACTION. When you find it, ask yourself: "Who or what performed that action?" The answer to that question will help you find the subject.

Example

Guns shoot.

The action word or verb here is *shoot*. Draw two lines under it, and ask yourself who or what shoots? The answer is *guns*, which is a noun. Draw one line under it. You have now located the subject and the predicate. Draw a line between them and you have separated the basic parts of this sentence. Follow these three steps as you do Exercise 1.

Separating Subjects and Predicates

EXERCISE 1

First Step.
Look for the verb, the word that expresses action, and draw two lines under it.

Second Step.
Look for the name of the person or thing that performs the action and draw one line under it.

Third Step.
Draw a line between these two words to separate the subject from the predicate. Write *S* over the subject, *P* over the predicate.

Example

S P
The dog / barked.

1. Fish swim.

2. Bees buzz.

3. Birds fly.

4. Babies cry.

5. Cats purr.

6. Trains run.

7. Planes fly.

8. Boats sail.

9. Wood burns.

10. Children play.

Notice that every sentence begins with a capital letter and ends with a period.

What you have just done is called "diagraming" a sentence. You have made a diagram of the main parts of the sentence. Now turn to the key of correct answers at the end of the book and go over your work. If you had no errors, you are ready to go on to Exercise 2. Always check your work after each exercise. If you make mistakes, go back and read the instructions again—until you are sure you understand them and know why you made errors.

In Exercise 2 you will notice that the sentences are longer. There may be more words than just the noun in the subject or just the verb in the predicate. We will learn about them later. Follow the same three steps as you diagram the sentences in Exercise 2.

EXERCISE 2

1. The snow fell.

2. A flower bloomed.

3. The girl cried.

4. The food smelled good.

5. A boy yelled.

6. The car speeds by.

7. The man whistled softly.

8. A girl laughed.

9. The bells rang loudly.

10. The clock struck ten.

Nouns as Subjects

Nouns are names. They are the names of people, places, or things. Words like *house, dog, tree, man, Washington, apple,* or *Saturday* are all nouns. Most nouns are preceded by *the* or *a*, but if a noun begins with a vowel sound (*a, e, i, o,* or *u*) it is preceded by *an*.

Examples

The man
A dog
An apple
The house
A tree
An umbrella
A shoe
The store
An idiot
The truth

We have seen that nouns are very important because they tell who or what is doing something. Every sentence must contain a noun which is the *subject* of the sentence. The subject is the person or thing which is performing the action.

Finding Subjects

EXERCISE 3

In the following exercise, draw a line under the subject of each sentence. If you have trouble, LOOK FOR THE ACTION! Then ask yourself who or what performed the action. Who played in sentence 1? What barked in sentence 2?

1. The boys played baseball.

2. A dog barked far away.

3. The car speeded past.

4. A policeman stopped it.

5. The driver looked unhappy.

6. The ticket cost him ten dollars.

7. An apple rolled off the table.

8. The women shopped for bargains.

9. Jimmy loves to fish.

10. An eagle soared across the sky.

Now look at the words you have underlined. Each one names people or things which are doing something. They are the subjects of the action taking place in the sentence.

Notice also that most of the nouns are preceded by *the* or *a*. *The* refers to certain definite subjects (e.g., the driver, the women); *a* or *an* refers to indefinite, nonspecific subjects. *A dog* is one of many dogs (see sentence 2), but *the boys* (sentence 1) refers to a specific group of boys. *An* is used before the two nouns, *apple* and *eagle*, which begin with vowels (*a, e, i, o,* or *u*). All other letters, all the hard sounds such as *d, t, k,* or *b*, are called consonants and are preceded by *a*.

EXERCISE 4

Draw a line under each subject.

1. The clouds gathered in the east.

2. A plane roared overhead.

3. The flowers wilted without water.

4. The telephone rang for a long time.

5. An ostrich has long legs.

6. The traffic grew much heavier.

7. Alice danced around the room.

8. An umbrella keeps off the rain.

9. The students did their homework.

10. A lady wrote to her son.

Check your answer key carefully. Did you find all the subjects? How many subjects were preceded by *a*? ___ How many by *an*? ___ Write the vowels at the beginnings of the words preceded by *an*. ________

Making up Subjects

EXERCISE 5

Make up your own subjects for the following incomplete sentences, and write them in the blank spaces. Be sure that the first word begins with a capital. Your subject must be a noun which refers to the person or thing performing the action described in the rest of the sentence.

When you have finished, diagram the completed sentence by underlining the verb twice, the subject once, and drawing a line between the subject and the predicate.

Example

__________ / ran down the street.

You might write in as subjects:

A dog

The thief

1. ________ walked into the pizza parlor.

2. ________ handed out hundred dollar bills.

3. ________ growled furiously outside the door.

4. ________ chased the frightened child.

5. ________ sits under a tree and dreams.

6. ________ drove a big blue Cadillac.

7. ________ dug deep into the soft earth.

8. ________ wore a crazy flowered hat.

9. __________ stalked across the empty stage.

10. __________ shouted angrily at the boy.

When you have finished, count how many of the subjects you wrote down are preceded by *the*. Record the number below. Then count how many are preceded by *a*. Make sure you have not used *a* before a word that begins with a vowel (*a*, *e*, *i*, *o*, or *u*). Write below the number of subjects preceded by *the*, by *a*, or by *an*.

The	*A*	*An*
______	_____	______

Verbs as Predicates

We have learned that it is not possible to construct a sensible sentence without having a noun which is the subject. In the same way, every sentence must also have a *verb* which tells what the subject does. Just as a locomotive pulls a train or an engine drives a car, so a verb supplies the action in a sentence.

Examples

Judy dances.
The dog barked.

We have seen that the part of the sentence which contains the verb is called the *predicate*. There may be more words than just the verb in the predicate.

Example

The dog/barked fiercely during the night.

Here the predicate contains not only the verb *barked* but also the word *fiercely* which tells *how* the dog barked and the phrase *during the night* which tells *when* the dog barked.

In the same way, the subject may also have words which describe or *modify* it, although the main subject can only be the noun which is the doer of the action expressed by the verb.

Example

Subject	Predicate
The huge, ferocious dog/	barked loudly.

In this sentence the *dog* is the doer; the other words describe or *modify* the *dog*. The verb is *barked*, although the complete predicate is *barked loudly*. The word *loudly* modifies the verb; it tells *how* the dog barked.

EXERCISE 6

Diagram the following sentences by underlining the verb twice, the subject once, and drawing a line between the subject and the complete predicate.

1. The boy dialed the wrong number.
2. The painter fell off the ladder.
3. The chef prepares a delicious meal.
4. The family ate dinner at the new restaurant.
5. A dog chases a squirrel in the park.
6. An artist drew a sketch of the old bridge.
7. The elephant escapes from the zoo.
8. An apple falls from the tree.
9. The dentist filled the cavity quickly.
10. The elevator stopped on the tenth floor.

When you diagram a sentence you map out its framework so that it becomes easy to see how the sentence is constructed. After you have checked your work with the answer key, read aloud the words you have underlined above. See how the main words in the sentence jump out at you so that you can easily see its basic structure. The other words, which we will study later, are all window dressing for the noun and verb which you have underlined.

Making up the Predicate

EXERCISE 7

Make up a predicate for each of the following

subjects and diagram the sentence as usual. Be sure you think of a verb which expresses some action the subject might be performing.

1. The hairy monster____________________.
2. An astronaut________________________.
3. The fat old lady______________________.
4. A green sports car ___________________.
5. The husky policeman__________________.
6. My grandmother _____________________.
7. The tall waiter_______________________.
8. The girl's blond hair__________________.
9. The frightened horse__________________.
10. The baseball team ____________________.

Review of Diagraming

EXERCISE 8

Every sentence must have:

1. A subject which performs the action. It is called a_______.
2. A predicate which describes the action the subject does. The main word is a_______.

Draw two lines under the verb or the word that expresses action. Then ask yourself who or what did this action? Find the *one* word that answers your question and draw a line under it. Draw a line between the noun and the verb and write *S* over the subject and *P* over the predicate.

1. Frank whistled.
2. The birds sang.
3. The employees ate lunch.
4. Our team won.
5. Mary fed her cat.
6. Joe dropped his hammer.
7. The clock stopped.
8. A bell rang.
9. The sun shone in the sky.
10. Flowers blossom in spring.
11. The moon rose across the lake.
12. The canoe glided down the river.
13. The red car roared down the street.
14. Ed hit the ball hard.
15. The boys played a game.
16. The passengers lined up quickly.
17. The supervisor handed out the paychecks.
18. The big black dog chased me away.
19. The goldfish swims around the pond.
20. The shining stars gleam in the sky.

Give yourself 5 points for each sentence you diagramed correctly. Take off 3 points for each error. What is your score? If it is 80 or more, go on to the next section. If it is lower than 80, go back and review what we have covered. Be sure you understand your mistakes before going on.

Simple and Complete Predicates

EXERCISE 9

We have already seen that the verb is the main word in the predicate, but not always the only word. Sometimes the predicate is a group of words.

Example

S P————————→
The dog / barked loudly at the boys.

In this case the verb is called the *simple predicate,* while the whole group of words, *barked loudly at the boys*, forms the *complete predicate*.

In the following sentences, locate the verb or simple predicate which describes the action and draw two lines under it. Then find the name of the subject that performs that action and draw one line under it. Write *S* over the subject, *P* over the verb or simple predicate, and separate them with a line. Draw arrows to show the complete predicate.

1. Fish swim all over the lake.
2. Bees buzz around the flowers all day.
3. Birds fly south in the winter.
4. Babies cry when they are hungry.
5. Cats purr deep down in their throats.
6. Trains run from Boston to California.
7. Planes fly very low over the airport.
8. Boats sail up and down the lake.
9. Plants need sunlight and water.
10. Children play in the park.

Stop and correct your work from the answer key before going on to Exercise 10. You will notice that in Exercise 9 all the subjects consist of only one word, while the complete predicates are quite long. In Exercise 10 the complete subject may contain other words which describe or *modify* the noun which is the subject. Diagram these sentences as you did in Exercise 9.

EXERCISE 10

1. The snow fell three feet deep last night.
2. A red flower bloomed in her garden.
3. The girl cried because she couldn't go.
4. The food smelled good to the hungry men.
5. A boy yelled at the big bully.
6. The foreign car speeds by with the police after it.
7. The man whistled softly to himself.
8. A girl laughed at his joke.
9. The church bells rang loudly on Sunday morning.
10. The clock struck ten in the empty old house.

Simple and Complete Subjects

EXERCISE 11

The subject, like the predicate, may be a group of words or a *phrase*. After you have located and underlined the *verb* or simple predicate twice, ask yourself: "Who or what performed this action?" Then underline once the *one* word which is the subject or the doer of that action. That word is called the *simple subject*. It is a *noun* which names the person or thing performing the action. The other words simply describe or tell you more about that noun, just as *big* and *yellow* describe the subject *dog* below.

Example

←——— S P ———→
The big yellow dog/barked loudly at the strangers.

In the following sentences, locate and underline the simple predicate or verb twice and the simple subject or noun once. Then separate and label the subject and predicate with arrows to show what words are included in the complete subject and complete predicate.

1. The big gray cat sat on the fence.
2. Thick white snowflakes drifted down.
3. A very tall boy ran across the street.
4. A big red car roared down the highway.

5. A police car speeded after it.

6. A fat old lady rocked the baby.

7. The shouting boys skated in the park.

8. A sleepy old man opened the door.

9. Two tired children crawled into bed.

10. The red-headed girl spells very well.

EXERCISE 12

You may have noticed by now that, although the simple subject is always a noun, not every noun is a subject. In Exercise 12, look at sentences 2, 3, 5, 7, 8, and 10. See how many nouns you can find in the predicate and list them below, after you have diagramed the sentences as you did in Exercise 11.

____________ ____________

____________ ____________

____________ ____________

____________ ____________

1. The young actor combed his hair.

2. My sister answered the telephone.

3. Our football team beat the other team.

4. Our coach praised our good playing.

5. The silent thief sneaked into the house.

6. The big watchdog barked at him.

7. A policeman drove his car up the street.

8. The sneaky thief ran away from the dog.

9. The policeman grabbed him as he ran.

10. The watchdog became the hero of the day.

Compound Subjects and Predicates

When a sentence has more than one subject for the same verb it is called a *compound subject.*

Example

Judy and Nancy / shopped in the department store.

When a sentence has more than one verb with the same subject it is called a *compound predicate* or a *compound verb.*

Example

The audience / laughed and applauded.

EXERCISE 13

Find subjects and predicates in the following sentences, underlining and separating them as usual. If there is a compound subject write CS above it. If there is a compound predicate write CP above it.

Example

C P
The dog / leaped and jumped.

C S
The men and women / crowded into the subway.

1. Rachel and Bill took a taxi home.

2. The audience cheers and claps for the actor.

3. Mike, Tom, and Betsy organized the meeting.

4. The young man slips and falls on the ice.

5. The car and the bike collided at the light.

6. The guests laugh and dance at the party.

7. Nancy and her sister left early.

8. They bought groceries and cooked dinner.

9. Mary opened the door and walked into the room.

10. Steve and his girl friend had an argument.

How many compound subjects did you find?____

How many compound predicates did you find?__

EXERCISE 14

Write sentences using the following *compound subjects:*

1. Beth and Jane________________________.

2. Ships and airplanes____________________.

3. Dogs and cats_________________________.

4. Thunder and lightning__________________.

5. Men and women_______________________.

Write sentences using the following *compound predicates:*

1. ___________danced and sang.

2. ___________run and jump.

3. ___________struggled and sweated.

4. ___________told jokes and played games.

5. ___________jumped into the water and swam.

Review Test of Subjects and Predicates

In the following sentences, locate and underline the simple predicate or verb twice and the simple subject or noun once. Separate and draw arrows over the complete subject and predicate. Label compound subjects *CS* and compound predicates *CP*.

EXERCISE 15

1. The frightened kitten crawled under the bed.
2. The cross old lady scolded the waiter.
3. Torn yellow curtains hung in the window.
4. The winter wind shrieked and howled down the alley.
5. Robins and bluejays sat in a tree.
6. The excited brown puppy ran around barking.
7. A beautiful girl bought the white satin dress.
8. The fat little boy and his brother ate the whole cake.
9. A train whistled loudly.
10. The train roared into the station.
11. The shining moon rose over the city.
12. A cherry tree bloomed in the park.
13. The winter rain poured down on the earth.
14. The thin man hurried down the street.
15. The angry dogs growled and barked at the stranger.
16. The hungry fish swim toward the bait.
17. The warm spring sun shone brightly.
18. The red sports car roared up the hill.
19. The very exciting game ended finally.
20. The noisy boys shouted and cheered.

Give yourself 5 points for each correctly diagramed sentence. Take off 2 points for each error. Did you score over 80? If so, go on to the next chapter after correcting your mistakes. If your score is less than 80, go back and reread the instructions; then do the exercises again. It is important that you understand each step before going on.

Chapter 2

More About Nouns

We have said that a noun is usually the name of a person, place, or thing. Sometimes it is a time, like *midnight*; or a season, like *autumn*; or an idea, like *democracy*. So far we have been looking at nouns only as subjects; but we have seen that sometimes there are other nouns in the sentences we have studied. A noun can be not only the *doer* of the verb's action, but it can also receive the action. In that case it is called the *object* of the action or the *object* of the verb.

Examples

SUBJECT	VERB	OBJECT
Jim	hit	Bill.
The boy	ate	the apple.
A dog	bit	the man.

In these sentences the action begins in the subject and ends in the object. The apple did not eat the boy, and Bill did not start the fight. The *object* answers the question "Who or what?" Jim hit (whom?). The boy ate (what?). A dog bit (what?). The noun which receives the action is called the *object of the verb*.

EXERCISE 16

Diagram the following sentences and label the parts *S* for the subject, *P* for the verb or simple predicate, and *O* for the object.

Example

S P O
Babies / drink milk.

1. The cat chased a mouse.
2. His mother called Tom.
3. My sister wore my dress.
4. The policeman grabbed the thief.
5. The firemen stopped the fire.
6. His car hit a tree.
7. The teacher graded the papers.
8. The mother rocked the baby.
9. The man paid his bill.
10. The wind rattles the windows.

Now stop and correct these sentences before going on to the harder ones in Exercise 17. Did you find the objects of action in each sentence?

EXERCISE 17

1. The dog gnawed his bone.
2. A bird sang a song.
3. The farmer planted seed.

4. Snow covered the ground.

5. The ship hit a reef.

6. The waves pounded the rocks.

7. A jet plane broke the sound barrier.

8. The capsule hit the ocean.

9. The rocket missed its target.

10. A bomb shattered the building.

Proper Nouns and Common Nouns

You have noticed that some nouns begin with capital letters and some do not. Nouns that refer to particular persons, places, or things are called *proper nouns*. They begin with capital letters. Ordinary nouns which refer to any one of a class of persons, places, or things are called *common nouns*. They do *not* begin with capital letters. For example, if you were writing about rivers in general, *rivers* would be a *common noun*. But if you were referring to the *Hudson River* you would begin with capitals because that is the name of a particular river. A proper noun always begins with a capital and is the name of a particular person, place, or thing. As you have seen, proper nouns sometimes contain more than one word: *Hudson River* or *Casey Stengel*.

In the following sentences, put a circle around each proper noun and an *X* above each common noun. Remember that the first word in a sentence has a capital but it may not be a proper noun.

Example

X

The (President) and his family live in the (White House.)

EXERCISE 18

1. Julie asked her mother for a quarter.

2. The fish swam around the pond.

3. Jonah was swallowed by a whale.

4. The little yellow bird sang in the tree.

5. June is my favorite month.

6. Robert moved to California.

7. His father bought a house in Los Angeles.

8. The picture fell off the wall.

9. Mary asked Grandmother to read her a story.

10. The dog bit the mailman.

Did you find 8 proper nouns, beginning with capitals? Did you find 15 common nouns? Check the answer key.

EXERCISE 19

1. Patty has a brother named David.

2. A little white rabbit ran across the yard.

3. Central Park is in New York.

4. Mary answered the telephone.

5. The children were going to school.

6. Don plays for the Mets.

7. Abe hit the ball with a stick.

8. The cheerful cook baked a big chocolate cake for Christmas Day.

9. My favorite sports are football, tennis, and track.

10. George, Joe, and Tony have parts in a show on Broadway.

Singular and Plural Nouns

Nouns may be singular or plural.

Singular nouns refer to one of anything.
a boy
the cat
an apple

Plural nouns refer to more than one. They usually end in *s* or *es*.
some boys
the three cats
a dozen apples

EXERCISE 20

Put a circle around each proper noun and an *X* above each common noun in the following sentences. Put an *S* over each singular noun and a *P* over each plural noun.

Example

S
The (Empire State Building) has over a
XP
hundred stories.

1. The girl bought a hat in the store.
2. The families of the Canadians waited at the airport.
3. The boys played ball with Billy.
4. My home is in Chicago, but I have a bungalow on Lake Erie.
5. Betty dropped a dish on the floor of the restaurant.
6. My cat chased Fido across the grass and down Elm Street.
7. On Sunday the fellows went to Shea Stadium.
8. The wolves howl on the mountains on cold winter nights.
9. John and his brother assembled the Volkswagen.
10. Those boys belong to Little League.

Did you find 20 common nouns? Did you find 12 proper nouns? Did you find 24 singular nouns? Did you find 7 plural nouns? Remember that every sentence begins with a capital, so not every word with a capital is a proper noun.

EXERCISE 21

Put a circle around each proper noun and an *X* above each common noun in the following sentences. Mark singulars and plurals with S or P.

1. George Washington was our first president.
2. Mark Twain and Washington Irving are famous American writers.
3. The Amazon is the longest river in South America.
4. The Giants won the game with the Jets last Saturday.
5. Sons often grow up to be like their fathers.
6. There are many pink flowers on the cherry tree.
7. One tulip bloomed in my garden.
8. Jupiter is a planet with several moons.
9. Venus and Mars are also planets.
10. We had beef and potatoes for dinner.

Irregular Plurals

The plural of nouns ending in *y* which have a vowel (*a*, *e*, *i*, *o*, or *u*) before the *y* is formed by adding *s*.

Examples

boy	boys
day	days

Nouns ending in *y* which do not have a vowel (*a*, *e*, *i*, *o*, or *u*) before the *y* form the plural by changing the *y* to *i* and then adding *es*.

Examples

baby	babies
cry	cries

EXERCISE 22

Form the plurals of these words ending in *y*.

1. toy ________________
2. body ________________
3. guy ________________
4. lady ________________
5. fly ________________
6. party ________________
7. sky ________________
8. key ________________
9. hobby ________________
10. story ________________

EXERCISE 23

Do you need more practice? Try these, looking at each one to see whether a vowel (*a*, *e*, *i*, *o*, or *u*) precedes the final *y*.

1. chimney ________________
2. company ________________
3. valley ________________
4. pony ________________
5. ray ________________
6. bunny ________________
7. family ________________
8. delay ________________
9. monkey ________________
10. candy ________________

The same rules apply to words ending in *o*. If the *o* is preceded by a vowel, the plural is formed just by adding *s*.

Examples

radio	radios
zoo	zoos

But words that end in *o* not preceded by a vowel form the plural by adding *es*.

Examples

hero	heroes
potato	potatoes

There are some exceptions to these rules, chiefly musical terms and musical instruments, where the plural is formed just by adding *s*.

Examples

banjo	banjos
solo	solos

EXERCISE 24

Form the plurals of the following words; use a dictionary if you are not sure.

PLURAL

1. trio ________________
2. tomato ________________
3. rodeo ________________
4. piano ________________
5. photo ________________
6. igloo ________________
7. embargo ________________
8. auto ________________
9. cargo ________________
10. hero ________________

Some words ending in *f* or *fe* change the *f* to *v* before adding the plural.

Examples

leaf	leaves
wife	wives

Learn the words in the examples and in the list below. You will then know most of the exceptions which form their plurals in this way.

SINGULAR	PLURAL
life	lives
elf	elves
loaf	loaves
calf	calves
shelf	shelves
thief	thieves
wolf	wolves
self	selves
sheaf	sheaves
half	halves
knife	knives

Some nouns have completely different forms in the plural. These are called *irregular nouns.* You will just have to memorize these, or look them up in the dictionary, since there is no rule which governs their spelling.

SINGULAR	PLURAL
mouse	mice
child	children
man	men
woman	women
foot	feet
goose	geese
ox	oxen
tooth	teeth
louse	lice
postman	postmen

The singular and plural forms of some nouns are the same.

Examples

sheep	moose
deer	trout
swine	bass

Collective Nouns

EXERCISE 25

Some nouns use the singular form to refer to a number of people or things. They are called *collective nouns* because they refer to a collection or a group.

Examples

An audience of listeners
A group of people
A troop of Boy Scouts
An army of soldiers
A flock of birds
A herd of sheep
A grove of trees
A church congregation

Write the proper collective noun on the line.

1. A__________of cows grazed in the meadow.
2. A__________of chickens was in the yard.

3. A_________of children played in the park.

4. The United States_________trains its officers at West Point.

5. The_________in the theater enjoyed the show.

6. The_________of the church attended Sunday services.

7. A_________of boys gathered on the street.

8. A_________of pine trees grew in the valley.

9. Our baseball ________ won the game.

10. My Boy Scout_________went on a hike.

Review of Singular and Plural Nouns

EXERCISE 26

For the plural nouns below, write their singular forms in the space provided.

	PLURAL	SINGULAR
1.	thieves	____________
2.	women	____________
3.	houses	____________
4.	mice	____________
5.	armies	____________
6.	nations	____________
7.	pianos	____________
8.	boxes	____________
9.	children	____________
10.	nurses	____________
11.	leaves	____________
12.	tomatoes	____________
13.	teeth	____________
14.	cabbages	____________
15.	horses	____________
16.	hobbies	____________
17.	lice	____________
18.	knives	____________
19.	knees	____________
20.	laces	____________

Review Test of Nouns

EXERCISE 27

A noun is the name of a__________________,

__________________, or__________________.

Nouns may be
1) common or proper.
2) singular or plural.
3) subject or object of the verb.

Diagram the following sentences as usual and circle the direct object if there is one.

Example
The boys / chased the (dog) down the street.

Always read back to yourself the marked words to see if they make sense. *Boys chased dog* expresses a complete thought and contains the sense of the sentence. *Boys chased street* does not make sense. In this case the noun *street* tells *where* the boys chased, not *what* they chased. The *dog* is the object because the dog received the action of being chased in the sentence.

1. Sally wears slacks to work.
2. The bird carried a worm to its nest.
3. Frank and Mario raced their cars down the highway.
4. A policeman drove his motorcycle after them.
5. The tall trooper gave a ticket to each of them.
6. A flock of ducks waddled across the road.
7. Sandy and Liz enjoyed the movie.
8. The children jumped and ran in the playground.
9. The sun rose from behind the mountains.
10. The American army won the battle.

Find examples of the following in the sentences above and write them in the spaces provided:

PROPER NOUNS	COMMON NOUNS
__________	__________
__________	__________
__________	__________
__________	__________
__________	__________

SINGULAR NOUNS	PLURAL NOUNS
__________	__________
__________	__________
__________	__________
__________	__________
__________	__________

Explain the following terms:

1. A compound subject____________________
______________________________.

2. A compound predicate____________________
______________________________.

3. A collective noun____________________
______________________________.

Diagram the following sentences as usual. Put a circle around any objects.

1. A robin built its nest in the tree.
2. The Bermans and the Shaws live in Chicago.
3. Julie and Pam led the parade.
4. The crowd shouted and screamed.
5. Our team won three football games.
6. A gang of boys broke windows in the school.
7. A policeman caught and arrested the fellows.
8. Our club elected a president named Joe Ferrara.
9. The astronauts walked in outer space.
10. The rocket reached the moon safely.

Fill the spaces below with examples of each of the following:

COMPOUND SUBJECT

____

____

COMPOUND PREDICATE

____

____

COLLECTIVE NOUNS

____

____

Find examples of the following nouns. (You may use the same noun more than once if you wish.)

PROPER	COMMON	SINGULAR	PLURAL
______	______	______	______
______	______	______	______
______	______	______	______
______	______	______	______
______	______	______	______

Give yourself 3 points for each correct sentence and 1 point for each space correctly filled. Take off 1 point for each mistake. If you are careful, you could get more than 100!

Chapter 3

Pronouns

Pronouns are little words that stand for nouns, just as movie stars have stand-ins. They always refer back to a previous noun; otherwise they make no sense.

Example

He took it to him.

This sentence has no meaning unless you know what the pronouns *he, it,* and *him* refer to.

Example

Bill's father asked Bill for the newspaper. He (Bill) took it (the paper) to him (Bill's father).

Pronouns are useful because they save us from a lot of tiresome repetition of the same words.

Example

Carl and Maria and Joe were late to work so they (Carl and Maria and Joe) reported to their boss. They (Carl and Maria and Joe) told him (the boss) that their (Carl's and Maria's and Joe's) subway had lost power and made them (Carl and Maria and Joe) late to work.

Pronouns are different from nouns because they change in form when they become objects.

Example

He (subject) called him (object).

The only pronouns that do not change in form are *you* and *it.* The forms of the others are given below.

SUBJECT	OBJECT	EXAMPLE
I	me	She likes me.
he	him	I like him.
she	her	He likes her.
we	us	They like us.
they	them	We like them.

EXERCISE 28

In each of the following sentences fill in the blank with the correct form of the pronoun, depending on whether it is a subject or an object.

1. Bill chased_________into the house. (I, me)

2. _________began to scream for my mother. (I, Me)

3. _________came running when she heard. (She, Her)

4. Joe and Harry came home for dinner with _________. (I, me)

5. My mother cooked a turkey for_________. (they, them)

6. After dinner__________all watched TV. (we, us)

7. Do you want to come with_________? (we, us)

8. __________are going to a show. (We, Us)

9. __________was wearing a new dress. (She, Her)

10. It looked beautiful on_________. (she, her)

You will note that in the above sentences there are little words such as *with, for,* and *on* which are followed by nouns ("for my mother" in sentence 2) or pronouns ("with me" in sentence 4). These little words are called *prepositions* and will be discussed later. They take nouns or pronouns as objects. So we say "with me," not "with I."

In Exercise 29, there are four prepositions, *to, with, between,* and *among,* which are also followed by objects.

When two pronouns are used in a compound subject, as in sentence 6, Exercise 29, it is polite usage always to refer to yourself last. The same rule applies to compound objects. Be careful to use the correct form of the pronoun, depending on whether it is a subject or an object.

Examples

My buddy and *I* (not *me*) went bowling.
The dog chased Eddie and *me* (not *I*).

Review Test of Pronouns

EXERCISE 29

In each of the following sentences fill in the blank with the correct form of the pronoun, depending on whether it is a subject or an object.

1. Polly and_________went swimming. (I, me)

2. _________ and Mary went to the movies. (He, Him)

3. They went with my boy friend and_____. (I, me)

4. Either Dan or_________will pick you up. (I, me)

5. You can go with__________if you want. (we, us)

6. __________and__________are buddies. (He, Him; I, me)

7. That's secret between you and_________. (I, me)

8. They have an agreement among_________. (they, them)

9. Both__________and__________were late to school. (she, her; I, me)

10. Was there a quarrel between_________ (she, her) and_________? (he, him)

Chapter 4

More About Verbs

We have said that verbs supply the action in a sentence, that they tell what it is the subject does. An action verb is like the engine that makes the train run; the verb makes the subject run, or perform in some way.

Verbs also tell at what time an action takes place. Verbs have different forms to express different times. These time forms are called *tenses*. There are three main tenses in English—*present, past,* and *future*. When the action is happening now, the verb is in the *present* tense.

Examples

I work hard on my job.
I hate to leave my girl friend.

When the action happened in the past, the verb is in the *past* tense. This is usually formed by adding *d* or *ed* to the verb.

Examples

I worked hard on my job.
I hated to leave my girl friend.

Actions in the future are formed by adding *will* to the verb.

Examples

I will work hard on my job.
I will hate to leave my girl friend.

In this case the verb is more than one word and is called a *verb phrase*. There are many helping words such as *have* or *should* or *might* that are used to express various times and shades of meaning.

Examples

I should have gone home.
Marie might have called me.
He had had a terrible experience.

We will not take up these more difficult forms of verbs in this book except to call them *verb phrases*. In such phrases the helping words change the meaning of the verb in some way. Thus, *will go* and *ought to go* do not mean the same as *go*.

Present and Past Tenses

EXERCISE 30

Form the past tense of the following verbs by adding *d* if the verb ends in *e* or *ed* if it does not. Words ending in *y* usually change the *y* to *i* before adding *ed*.

Examples

Present	*Past*
love	loved
fill	filled
try	tried

Say to yourself: "Today, I walk. Yesterday, I walked," etc.

PRESENT TENSE	PAST TENSE
1. skate	____________
2. study	____________
3. buzz	____________
4. bloom	____________
5. whistle	____________
6. light	____________
7. laugh	____________
8. cry	____________
9. marry	____________
10. wash	____________

EXERCISE 31

Write the present tense of each of the verbs given below in the space provided.

PRESENT TENSE	PAST TENSE
1. ____________	wished
2. ____________	asked
3. ____________	liked
4. ____________	tried
5. ____________	dropped
6. ____________	planted
7. ____________	washed
8. ____________	noted
9. ____________	chased
10. ____________	provided

EXERCISE 32

When we are speaking of another person or thing performing the action, the verb ends in *s* or *es*. Again, change the final *y* to *i* before adding the ending.

Examples

I run.	He runs.
I cry.	She cries.

Write the proper ending for the following verbs. Say to yourself: "He (she or it) raises."

1. raise	He	____________
2. dress	She	____________
3. hate	He	____________
4. brush	She	____________
5. fry	He	____________
6. smile	She	____________
7. want	He	____________
8. carry	She	____________
9. push	It	____________
10. wait	He	____________

Write the past tense of the following verbs. Say to yourself: "Today he (she or it) raises. Yesterday he raised."

1. raises	____________
2. dresses	____________
3. hates	____________
4. brushes	____________
5. fries	____________
6. smiles	____________

7. wants ____________

8. pushes ____________

9. waits ____________

10. carries ____________

EXERCISE 33

Write the present tense of each of the verbs given below in the space provided.

1. ____________ He waited.

2. ____________ It required.

3. ____________ She rushed.

4. ____________ He demanded.

5. ____________ She cried.

6. ____________ He screamed.

7. ____________ It mated.

8. ____________ He killed.

9. ____________ It moved.

10. ____________ He fired.

Irregular Verbs

EXERCISE 34

Many verbs in English change their forms when they change their tense.

Example
Today I ring the bell. Yesterday I rang the bell.

There are no rules for these verbs, which are called *irregular*. Many of them come to us from the language of the ancient Anglo-Saxons from which English is descended. The correct forms are usually learned when a child learns to talk. If you say each verb to yourself in sentences like the ones above, you can usually tell whether it sounds correct. If you aren't sure, look it up in a dictionary which gives the past tense.

Write the past tense of each verb given in the space provided. Be sure to say to yourself: "Today I________. Yesterday I________."

PRESENT	PAST
1. take	____________
2. run	____________
3. eat	____________
4. go	____________
5. come	____________
6. grow	____________
7. speak	____________
8. fight	____________
9. hit	____________
10. fall	____________
11. fly	____________
12. swim	____________
13. tell	____________
14. sing	____________
15. make	____________
16. rise	____________
17. shine	____________
18. win	____________
19. feed	____________
20. drink	____________

Make a list of any of these irregular forms you do not know and memorize them. Then try Exercise 35. Repeat these exercises until you are sure of all the irregular forms.

EXERCISE 35

Write the present tense of each of the following verbs in the space provided, making the subject another person. Say to yourself: "Yesterday he wrote. Today he writes."

1. ____________ wrote
2. ____________ won
3. ____________ shot
4. ____________ came
5. ____________ went
6. ____________ sat
7. ____________ broke
8. ____________ rose
9. ____________ swam
10. ____________ bought
11. ____________ shone
12. ____________ slept
13. ____________ told
14. ____________ lit
15. ____________ caught
16. ____________ bent
17. ____________ fed
18. ____________ held
19. ____________ took
20. ____________ thought

Verbs of Being

Verbs are not always *action* words. There are also verbs of *being*, the most common of which are *am*, *are*, *is*, *was*, and *were*. These verbs express no action, only a state of being. They are like equal signs in arithmetic.

Examples

Betsy is a girl.
Betsy = a girl.

I am your father.
I = your father.

Verbs of being are irregular. They change in form to agree with the subject. The subject may be a noun or a pronoun, the little word which acts as a stand-in for a noun.

PRESENT	PAST
I am	I was
You are	You were
He, she, or it is	He, she, or it was
We are	We were
You are	You were
They are	They were

EXERCISE 36

Diagram the following sentences in the usual way, with two lines under the verb of being, one line under the simple subject, and a vertical line separating the complete subject from the complete predicate. Label the two parts S or P.

Example
S P
The women / were late to work.

1. Celeste is a pretty girl.
2. The dog was black and white.

3. I am hungry for supper.

4. The men are outdoors.

5. The train was late tonight.

6. The stars were bright in the sky.

7. This horse is very smart.

8. The audience was too noisy.

9. I am glad to see my friend.

10. The women were in the office.

EXERCISE 37

Fill in a verb of being in each of the following sentences.

1. Richie__________the best pitcher.

2. Jim and Doug__________catchers on our team.

3. Julie Andrews__________the star in *Mary Poppins.*

4. At night I__________sleepy.

5. You think you__________so smart!

6. Yesterday you__________late to work.

7. Last summer Tim__________working.

8. Now he__________back in school.

9. This week my brother__________home on leave from the army.

10. Where__________you going tomorrow?

Pronouns with Verbs of Being

The most common verbs of being are *am, are, is, was,* and *were*. Memorize these five little words because they are used very frequently. Verbs of being do not express action; they simply act like equal signs between the subject and the predicate. The predicate after a verb of being describes the subject or tells you something about it.

Examples

My name is Sue Jackson.
My name = Sue Jackson.

The boys are members of the team.
The boys = members of the team.

EXERCISE 38

Diagram the following sentences, but say to yourself: "Who or what is the subject?" instead of "Who or what does the action?"

1. She was very mean to me.

2. They are not nice to strangers.

3. Our family is together on weekends.

4. We were at the beach last Sunday.

5. The weather was very hot.

6. It was almost too hot to walk on the sand.

7. The waves were very powerful.

8. Sometimes people are not very thoughtful.

9. They were often at home.

10. I am pleased with your progress.

Find six pronoun subjects in the sentences above. Write them on the lines below.

1. __________ 4. __________

2. __________ 5. __________

3. __________ 6. __________

EXERCISE 39

In the following sentences, write in the correct verb of being above the *equal* sign.

1. I = hungry.
2. He = my brother.
3. The boys = members of the baseball team.
4. Last year they = the high school champions.
5. She = the best student in the class.
6. We = very good friends.
7. We = watching TV at my house last night.
8. My mother = going out shopping.
9. Last year our coach = Chuck Wilson.
10. He = a very good coach all that year.

Verbs Preceding Their Subjects

EXERCISE 40

The subject of the sentence does not always come before the predicate. Sometimes the subject comes last in the sentence.

Always find the verb first. Then ask yourself who or what did the action or had being and you will find the subject.

Diagram the following sentences in the usual manner. After each sentence write *Pr* if it is in the present tense, *P* if it is in the past tense.

Example

In the east shone / a bright star. P

1. In the last row sits John.________________
2. At the back of the room was a huge fireplace.
____
3. Under my window grows a beautiful rose-bush.______________________________
4. On the porch in a rocking chair sat the old, old lady.____________________________
5. After all the cold weather comes the warm, lovely spring.__________________________
6. Next to my house is a little park. ____________
7. Down the chimney came Santa Claus!_______
8. After the dinner came a delicious dessert._____
9. Inside all the tissue paper was a tiny gold box.
____
10. Last of all, after everybody else, came Peter!
____

EXERCISE 41

In these sentences you may find the subject anywhere in the sentence. Diagram in the usual manner, marking S and P where needed. Circle any objects of verbs. You should find five objects.

1. Next to the wall the children planted flowers.
2. With great caution the robber opened the window.
3. Under the trees in the shade sat the old man.
4. With a terrible roar, the jet passed overhead.
5. After lunch the brothers went shopping.
6. Last of all comes the grand prize.
7. On Saturday we took a trip to Connecticut.
8. Barking angrily, the dog charged the stranger.
9. Smiling sweetly, the lady opened the door for the guests.
10. After the storm came the sunshine again.

Predicate Nouns

Verbs of being do not express action. Therefore they do not take objects, since no action is received. Nouns that follow a verb of being are called *predicate nouns*. They are simply another name for the subject.

Example

Jim Grillo is my brother.

There is no action here. *Brother* is simply another name for *Jim Grillo*. Since it is in the predicate, it is called the *predicate noun*.

Example

The boy ate the apple.

Remember that an object receives the action of the verb. In this sentence, *apple* is the object of the verb *ate*. For a review of objects, go back and do Exercise 16 again.

Diagram the following sentences in the usual manner and write *O* above the object. In sentences using verbs of being, write *PN* (predicate noun) above the noun in the predicate which describes or tells you something about the subject.

Examples

S P O
John / kicked the football.

S P PN
John / is the quarterback.

EXERCISE 42

1. The boys caught a fish.
2. My grandmother is Mrs. Wilson.
3. Jimmy hit a foul ball.
4. Mary is the oldest person here.
5. I am your new supervisor.
6. The boy slammed the door.
7. You are the last one to finish.
8. Joe carried the garbage can outside.
9. Tom shoveled the driveway for me.
10. The students did their work quickly.

How many predicate nouns did you find?

After a verb of being, a pronoun in the predicate is, like a noun, a *predicate pronoun*. In this case, the pronoun keeps the form of a subject.

Examples

It is he who called me.
It was they who started the fight.

The expression "It's me," while not correct in grammar, is widely used and is accepted nowadays. Actually, the correct expression would be "It's I," with the predicate pronoun *I* following the verb of being *is*.

EXERCISE 43

Follow the same directions as for Exercise 42.

1. John is a good friend of mine.
2. He opened the package from his sister.
3. Janet left her purse at home.
4. That desk is an antique.
5. We gave a party for the couple.
6. She is a reporter for the local newspaper.
7. They built their house themselves.
8. Bruce feeds his cat three times a day.
9. You are an excellent writer.
10. I am the best cook in my family.

Review of Verbs

Verbs that tell about what is happening now are

in the present time or *present tense.*

Verbs that tell what happened in the past are in the *past tense.* Most verbs form the past tense by adding *d* (as in pok*ed*) or *ed* (as in sand*ed*).

Beside each verb below, write its past tense. Say to yourself: "Today I . . . . (dance). Yesterday I . . . . (danced)."

EXERCISE 44

PRESENT	PAST
1. wash	______
2. fill	______
3. twist	______
4. dress	______
5. choke	______
6. mend	______
7. rain	______
8. land	______
9. mail	______
10. test	______

Verbs of being change in form to agree with the subject. The five verbs of being are:

1. ______
2. ______
3. ______
4. ______
5. ______

EXERCISE 45

Write the correct form of the present and past tense of the verbs of being for the subjects below.

PRESENT		PAST	
1. I	______	7. He	______
2. She	______	8. I	______
3. You	______	9. We	______
4. We	______	10. She	______
5. They	______	11. You	______
6. It	______	12. They	______

EXERCISE 46

Verbs that have a different form in the past tense are called *irregular* verbs. Write the past tense for each verb below.

PRESENT	PAST
1. dig	______
2. run	______
3. sing	______
4. think	______
5. fly	______
6. sit	______
7. drink	______
8. win	______
9. bring	______
10. sink	______

Can you think of more irregular verbs? Write them in the spaces below. (See Exercises 34 and 35.)

11. ______	______
12. ______	______
13. ______	______

14. ____________ ____________

EXERCISE 47

What is wrong with the following sentences? Can you correct them?

Example
I started the car and drive down the street.
(Corrected)
I started the car and drove down the street.

Use the first verb in the sentence to determine the tense of the second verb.

1. First we eat breakfast and then we went to school.
2. Mary cut Anne's hair and curls it.
3. The mother fed and changes the baby.
4. You wash the dishes and I dried them.
5. We ate and drink well.
6. The boys fight and yelled at each other.
7. The policeman stops his car and walked over to the boys.
8. The fire engine roared down the street and skids around the corner.
9. I went to the movies and then I come home.
10. I am in a hurry but he was not.

Review Test of Verbs

EXERCISE 48

A. Diagram the following sentences.

1. The three boys fished all day in the river.
2. Bass, pickerel, and trout were their catch.
3. Low in the sky sank the sun.
4. The evening shadows crept across the valley.
5. Home went the boys with their catch.
6. Their supper that night was delicious fresh fish.
7. Tim, Jack, and Joe were old friends.
8. They often went fishing together.
9. One day they saw a school of pickerel.
10. Now they watch the river every day.

B. In the sentences above, find examples of the following.

1. A proper noun ____________
2. A common singular noun ____________
3. A collective noun ____________
4. A verb of being ____________
5. A verb of action in the past tense ____________
6. A direct object ____________
7. A compound subject ____________
8. A pronoun ____________
9. A verb in the present tense ____________
10. A predicate noun ____________

C. Write the singular or the plural of each of the following nouns.

SINGULAR	PLURAL
1. woman	____________
2. lady	____________

3. boy ____________

4. wish ____________

5. gentleman ____________

6. ____________ mice

7. ____________ houses

8. ____________ geese

9. ____________ days

10. ____________ knives

D. Write the past or present tense of each verb below.

PRESENT	PAST
1. wash	____________
2. go	____________
3. fly	____________
4. sing	____________
5. think	____________
6. am	____________
7. want	____________
8. creep	____________
9. watch	____________
10. run	____________
11. ____________	wandered
12. ____________	rang
13. ____________	bought
14. ____________	were
15. ____________	swam
16. ____________	stopped
17. ____________	was
18. ____________	belonged
19. ____________	wore
20. ____________	blossomed

E. Put a suitable pronoun before each of these verbs of being.

1. ____________ am

2. ____________ was

3. ____________ were

4. ____________ are

5. ____________ is

F. Put a suitable verb of being in each of the following spaces.

1. Yesterday he __________ here.

2. Tomorrow I __________ going home.

3. They __________ at the picnic last week.

4. She __________ the happiest person I know.

5. We __________ leaving right now.

Give yourself 5 points for each sentence correctly diagramed. Take 2 points off for each error. Give yourself 1 point for each item on the rest of the test. Did you get at least 80? If not, go back and review your mistakes.

Chapter 5

Four Kinds of Sentences

So far we have been talking about the most common type of sentence: *a statement* of some kind. A sentence that makes a statement always ends with a period.

Example

This is Monday, June 5.

There are also other kinds of sentences. *Questions* are easy to spot. They usually begin with the verb and always end with a question mark.

Example

Is this Monday?

Exclamations express excitement or emotion of some kind and end with an exclamation mark.

Example

What a terrible thing to do!

The fourth and last kind of sentence is the *command.* It may begin with "please," but it is still a request or an order. The subject (you) is usually implied rather than stated.

Examples

(You) Stand up straight.
Please (you) pass the salt.

These periods, exclamation marks, and question marks are called *punctuation.* The same sentence with different punctuation expresses different meanings.

Examples
Joe hit Jim. *Statement*
(Did) Joe hit Jim? *Question*
Joe, hit Jim. *Command*
Joe hit Jim! *Exclamation*

Marie has done her work. *Statement*
Marie, have you done your work? *Question*
Marie, (you) do your work. *Command*
Marie did her work! *Exclamation*

Statements and Questions

EXERCISE 49

A sentence is a group of words expressing a complete thought. A sentence which makes a statement begins with a capital and is followed by a period.

Example

The janitor went to the door.

A sentence which asks a question begins with a capital and is followed by a question mark.

Example

Where did the janitor go?

Read each of the following sentences and after it write *S* if it is a statement and *Q* if it is a question. Put a period or question mark after each sentence.

1. What do you want ____________________
2. I want to go with you ________________
3. Jim hit John ________________________
4. Why did he do that __________________
5. It was not John's fault _______________
6. Jim has a nasty temper _______________
7. Where are you going _________________
8. I am going to work __________________
9. Do you like your boss ________________
10. No, he is too crabby ________________

How many questions did you find? __________

EXERCISE 50

Read each of the following sentences and after it write *S* if it is a statement and *Q* if it is a question. Put a period or question mark after each sentence.

1. What shall we do now ________________
2. Shall we go fishing __________________
3. No, I don't feel like fishing ____________
4. Would you like some ice cream __________
5. This is good, isn't it ________________
6. Tomorrow is my day off _______________
7. What will you do ____________________
8. I hope it doesn't rain ________________
9. I have to paint the house ______________
10. Wouldn't you like to help me ___________

Commands and Exclamations

EXERCISE 51

Besides *statements* and *questions* there are two more kinds of sentences.

1. A *command* begins with a capital and ends with a period, like a statement.
   The subject is always *you*, but it is often left out.

   (You) Keep off the grass.
   (You) Pass the butter, please.

2. A sentence that expresses excitement or strong feeling is called an *exclamation*. It begins with a capital and ends with an exclamation mark.

   Something terrible has happened!
   Hurry! We need the doctor!

After each of the following sentences write *C* for command or *E* for exclamation.

1. Go on home now. ____________________
2. Oh! I forgot something! ______________
3. Turn off the headlights. ______________
4. Quick! Call the police! _______________
5. Please shut the door. ________________
6. Don't walk on the grass. ______________

7. Hey! Guess what happened! ___________

8. Call me up tonight. ___________

9. Long live the king! ___________

10. Please pass in your papers. ___________

EXERCISE 52

After each of the following sentences write *C* for command or *E* for exclamation. Add (you) before the verb in each command.

1. Hand me that book. ___________

2. Hear this. Now hear this. ___________

3. What a wonderful idea! ___________

4. Gee, that would be great! ___________

5. Please tell me what happened. ___________

6. It's a deep, dark secret! ___________

7. Turn right at the corner. ___________

8. Holy cow, look at that! ___________

9. Get a move on, you guys. ___________

10. Get going before you get caught. ___________

Identifying Sentences

EXERCISE 53

The four kinds of sentences begin with capitals and end with periods, question marks, or exclamation marks.

Question	?
Statement	.
Command (You)	.
Exclamation	!

Tell what kind of sentence each of the following is by writing the correct letter after it: *Q* for question, *S* for statement, *C* for command, and *E* for exclamation.

1. What time is it? ___________

2. Drop that gun. ___________

3. George was late to work. ___________

4. Nina, come here at once. ___________

5. Don't you think Patty reads well? ___________

6. The telephone rang for a long time. ___________

7. How fast the children ran! ___________

8. Please put it on the table. ___________

9. May I borrow that book? ___________

10. Joe needs another pencil. ___________

EXERCISE 54

Tell what kind of sentence each of the following is by writing the correct letter after it: *Q* for question, *S* for statement, *C* for command, and *E* for exclamation.

1. Come in, please. ___________

2. Why are you late? ___________

3. Quick, call a doctor. ___________

4. That is a pretty dress. ___________

5. Do you like it? ___________

6. I think it's lovely! ___________

7. It is time for lunch. ___________

8. Do you like to swim? ___________

9. Close that window. ___________

10. It's a beautiful day.____________________

Review Test of Sentences

EXERCISE 55

A. Write the correct word in the blank.

1. What kind of sentence ends with a question mark?____________________
2. What kind of sentence makes a statement of fact?____________________
3. What kind of sentence has an implied subject *You*?____________________
4. What kind of sentence expresses excitement?____________________
5. What must every sentence begin with?

____

B. Put in capitals and punctuation and tell what kind of sentence each of the following is.

1. please pass the butter______________
2. why are you so late______________
3. it is much colder tonight______________
4. my goodness, what a surprise ______
5. what happened______________
6. somebody got hurt______________
7. gosh, that's terrible______________
8. did you call a doctor______________
9. help, call the police______________
10. they're already here______________

C. Punctuate and tell what kind of sentence each of the following is.

1. what time is it______________
2. it is seven o'clock______________
3. pass the bread, please______________
4. it is time for bed______________
5. get to bed, boys ______________
6. Henry broke his leg______________
7. how did he do that______________
8. quick, get a doctor______________
9. get Dr. Fox on the telephone________
10. he's coming right over______________
11. what are you doing______________
12. it's none of your business__________
13. don't get fresh with me____________
14. are you looking for trouble_________
15. gosh, you must be nuts____________
16. why don't you get lost_____________
17. I have a sore throat______________
18. get out of the way ______________
19. do you think you can win _________
20. ouch, that hurt______________

Give yourself 2 points for each sentence in A and 3 points for those in B and C. Take off 1 point for each mistake. Did you get at least 80? Do you understand your errors?

Chapter 6

Complete and Incomplete Sentences

We have now learned a good deal about sentences. We have seen that every sentence

1. Is made up of a subject and a predicate.
2. Contains a noun or pronoun which is the main word in the subject.
3. Contains a verb of action or being which is the main word in the predicate.
4. Begins with a capital letter and ends with a period, question mark, or exclamation mark.

We have also studied the structure of sentences through diagraming, and we know that verbs of action are often followed by objects which receive that action.

Example

The batter hit the ball.

Verbs of being, on the other hand, are followed by predicate nouns which are simply a way of describing the subject.

Examples

I am an engineer.
My brother is a Democrat.

We know also that there are different kinds of sentences (statements, commands, questions, and exclamations) but that all correct sentences must express a complete thought. Many beginners have difficulty with this. They have not learned that sentences must have a subject and a predicate and express one complete thought. Frequently, several complete thoughts are strung together in what are called *run-on sentences*.

Example

Jerry and I went to the drugstore for
a soda we stayed there all afternoon.

This should be two separate sentences since it expresses two different complete thoughts.

Jerry and I went to the drugstore for a soda.
We stayed there all afternoon.

Another common error is the *incomplete sentence*, which does not have a subject or a predicate, or is unfinished in meaning.

Example

When we went out to lunch.

The reader never knows what happened at lunch. In order to avoid such errors, remember always to ask yourself:

"What is the action taking place?"

"Who or what performs that action?"

If your sentence contains these basic requirements, it expresses a complete thought.

Complete Sentences

EXERCISE 56

A sentence expresses a complete thought. It begins with a captial and ends with a period. If the sentence asks a question, it ends with a question mark instead of a period. If it expresses excitement, it is followed by an exclamation mark instead of a period. These marks are called *punctuation*.

Read the following groups of words and draw a line through each one that is not a complete thought.

Put a capital letter at the beginning and the proper punctuation at the end of each one which is a complete sentence.

Example A walked into the house
This is not a complete sentence because it does not tell you *who* walked in. Therefore a line should be drawn through it.

Example B the boys walked into the house
This expresses a complete thought so it should begin with a capital and end with a period.
The boys walked into the house.

1. went down the street
2. two girls went down the street
3. they waited on the corner
4. running down the path
5. when she went in the house
6. suddenly a voice
7. suddenly Nancy heard a voice
8. in the gray light of dawn
9. the boys went fishing
10. and ran to the window

How many complete sentences did you find?_____

EXERCISE 57

Read the following groups of words and draw a line through each one that is not a complete thought. Put a capital letter at the beginning and the proper punctuation at the end of each one which is a complete sentence.

1. three cars are
2. three cars are colliding
3. the cop on the corner
4. the cop on the corner has a gun
5. after my lunch
6. soon the bell rang
7. turned on the light
8. my mother turned on the light
9. when the doorbell rang
10. when the doorbell rang I opened the door

Incomplete Sentences

EXERCISE 58

The following are *not* complete sentences. On the line under each group of words, write a sentence using these words to express a complete thought.

1. when the siren sounded

____

____

2. rushing downstairs, Sally

____

____

3. Norman said that he

____

____

4. and sat down to watch TV

5. on a hot summer day

6. like to swim

7. John and Bill also

8. rang again and again

9. up the ladder

10. later in the day

Did you remember the capitals at the beginning?

EXERCISE 59

The following are *not* complete sentences. On the line under each group of words, write a sentence using these words to express a complete thought.

1. ran into the house

2. the lamp on the table

3. my lunch at work

4. I wish I had taken

5. too cold to go

6. right after breakfast

7. standing quietly in the corner

8. their friends and relatives

9. before dark

10. it was very

Run-on Sentences

EXERCISE 60

A sentence is a group of words which expresses only one complete thought. Different thoughts should be separated from each other in different sentences, not strung together in one. This common mistake is called a *run-on sentence.*

In the examples below, make each run-on sentence into two or three separate sentences, each one containing a complete thought, by using capitals and punctuation correctly.

Example

Tom came home he had supper his brother and he went out to play ball

This should be:

Tom came home. He had supper. His brother and he went out to play ball.

1. your letter came yesterday I read it afterwards I showed it to my buddy

2. his umbrella blew away in the wind it went flying down the street

3. the cat was angry she started clawing me then I hit her

4. my wife asked me to go to the store I forgot all about it

5. someone called my name I turned around there was my friend Joe

6. I read about him in the paper it said he was a great pitcher

7. Jim wanted to go to the movies his girl friend wanted to go dancing

8. a big plane was flying over the house suddenly we heard an explosion we ran outside

9. all we could see was dust then suddenly flames sprang up

10. people were screaming I tried to get close the flames were too hot

There are 25 complete thoughts in the sentences above. Did you find them all? Count your sentences.

EXERCISE 61

Follow the same directions as for Exercise 60.

1. after the show we went to the drugstore we each had a Coke

2. yesterday was my mother's birthday I forgot to buy her a present

3. he heard a noise it was outside his window

4. when she left work it was raining she took a taxi home

5. it's too cold in here I think I'll get my sweater

6. my brother asked me to drive him to work I couldn't because my car was being repaired

7. last night we came home late we got caught in a traffic jam

8. I wish I had a bike then I could ride to work

9. she starts her new job this week I hope she likes it

10. maybe they will visit us soon we enjoy their company

How many sentences did you find?__________

Review Test of Sentences

EXERCISE 62

A. 1. What is a sentence?

____

2. What are the two parts of a sentence?

____

3. What must a sentence begin with?

____

4. What must a sentence end with?

____

5. What is a run-on sentence?

____

B. The following include complete sentences, incomplete sentences, and run-on sentences.

a.) Punctuate the complete sentences.

b.) Draw a line through the incomplete sentences.

c.) Separate the run-on sentences and punctuate properly.

1. where are you going, my pretty maid
2. after we go to the show
3. I would like a drink of water
4. he went to work then he came home for dinner
5. because it is so hot
6. first she wrote the report after that she went to the meeting
7. after all that, she was tired out
8. he's a big tall guy with red hair
9. although he gets his work done
10. first he did setting-up exercises then he took a hot shower

C. Make sentences using these groups of words and write them on the lines below. Be sure to use capitals, question marks, or exclamation marks where needed.

1. my father and I
2. where did you
3. the planet Mars
4. oh, my goodness
5. ran faster than ever
6. why were they
7. the people in our car pool
8. out of the window
9. fell flat on his face
10. the teacher's dress
11. when did she
12. the fellows in this block
13. ran down the street
14. with the siren screaming
15. good heavens
16. what is that
17. the last thing
18. did he ask
19. out the window
20. why in the world

Give yourself 3 points for each sentence in B and C, 2 points each for A. Check your own capitals and punctuation in C.

Chapter 7

Punctuation

Correct punctuation is very important in writing. Punctuation can change the whole meaning of a sentence.

Examples

Don hit him.
Don, hit him!

A comma, as in the sentence above, indicates a pause, and is used to separate or set off the name of the person spoken to. That sentence is really a command, with *you* as the implied subject.

Example

Don, (you) hit him!

Commas are also used to separate quotations of what people say from the rest of the sentence.

Example

Jim said, "Let's go swimming."
or
"Let's go swimming," said Jim.

Note that if the quotation precedes the rest of the sentence, it ends with a comma rather than a period because the sentence is not complete. Quotation marks turn in toward the words which are being quoted: " before the beginning and " after the comma or period which ends the quotation.

Quotations

There are three things to remember about quotations.

1. Whenever a person's words are repeated exactly they must be set off from the rest of the sentence by quotation marks *before* and *after* them.
2. The quotation must begin with a capital, and it must end with a period if it ends the sentence.
3. The quotation must be separated from the rest of the sentence by a comma.

EXERCISE 63

Place commas, periods, and quotation marks in the right places.

Example

Marie said, "My kitten is black and white."

1. The supervisor said Let's start our meeting
2. Alex announced Our new cleaning products are very popular
3. Mary stated We made a large profit from them in the first six months
4. Susan remarked They sell best in the Middle West
5. Bill replied That's where we have done the most advertising
6. Mary suggested We need more radio ads in

other parts of the country

7. Alex said It's important to find out why our customers prefer our products

8. Susan said Let's make a survey of our customers in the Middle West

9. Bill answered That's a great idea

10. The supervisor said Now we'll discuss those radio ads

EXERCISE 64

In the following sentences put in punctuation (commas, periods, and quotation marks) and change lower case letters to capitals where needed.

1. Sarah announced I'd like to go camping for our vacation
2. Bob said that's impossible because we don't have any camping equipment
3. Sarah answered we could borrow the Nelsons' equipment
4. Bob said OK, but we need to decide where we're going
5. Sarah suggested I think Ontario would be a lovely place to camp
6. Bob sighed yes, but that would be a long drive
7. Sarah replied well, we could camp along the way
8. Bob said but we have only two weeks of vacation
9. Sarah said I guess that isn't enough time
10. Bob suggested we could camp at one of the state parks near here

EXERCISE 65

Sometimes the quotation comes first in a sentence. In that case, instead of a period at the end of the quotation, a comma is used to separate it from the rest of the sentence.

Example

"I love football," said Bernie.

Put commas, quotation marks, and periods in the right places.

1. I got a raise announced Sally at dinner
2. I'm very pleased to hear it exclaimed her mother
3. You've worked very hard for that said her father
4. I think this calls for a celebration he added
5. I think so, too Sally's mother said
6. I don't see anything so great about it growled her brother
7. That's just because you're jealous snapped back Sally
8. Now don't quarrel at dinner said their mother
9. I was going to suggest a treat for all of us their father remarked
10. In that case, it's OK with me announced Sally's brother

EXERCISE 66

Put in punctuation and capitals as above. In this exercise, the quotation may come before or after the rest of the sentence. See how much more interesting the story sounds than it did in Exercise 64.

1. I'd like to go camping for our vacation Sarah announced
2. Bob said that's impossible because we don't have any camping equipment

3. We could borrow the Nelsons' equipment Sarah answered

4. Bob said OK, but we need to decide where we're going

5. Sarah suggested I think Ontario would be a lovely place to camp

6. Yes, but that would be a long drive Bob sighed

7. Sarah replied well, we could camp along the way

8. But we have only two weeks of vacation Bob said

9. Sarah said I guess that isn't enough time

10. We could camp at one of the state parks near here Bob suggested

Questions and Exclamations in Quotations

Like ordinary sentences, quotations may end in question marks or exclamation marks instead of periods. If such a quotation comes at the beginning of a sentence, it does *not* need a comma to separate it from the rest of the sentence. The question mark or exclamation mark is enough punctuation.

Examples

"Hello!" called the cheerful lady.
"How are you today?" she said, smiling.

EXERCISE 67

Punctuate the following and insert quotation marks in the right places.

1. Where are you going asked the young woman

2. I'm going running answered the young man

3. Can I come with you she asked

4. Of course you can he exclaimed

5. I like having company when I run he added

6. Oh, and I love the exercise said the young woman

7. When did you start running asked the young man

8. I started about two years ago she said

9. I wanted to keep in shape she added

10. Come on, let's go he said

EXERCISE 68

Sometimes a person says more than one thing at a time. You may have a quotation of two or more sentences, with the reference to the person who is speaking coming between the quotations.

Example

"Turn off that radio," said my father. "I can't hear myself think!"

Punctuate the following sentences.

1. Where am I asked the bearded man

2. You are in the hospital said the nurse

3. The hospital Good heavens exclaimed the man

4. Now, don't get excited the nurse said We will take good care of you

5. What happened to me asked the man

6. You were hit by a car said the nurse Don't you remember anything

7. I remember riding my motorcycle the man

said I don't know what happened after that

8. Am I going to get well he asked

9. Of course you are exclaimed the nurse The doctor will soon be here

10. Thank goodness for that sighed the man

Review Test of Punctuation

EXERCISE 69

Every sentence begins with a capital and ends with a period. Questions end with a question mark, and exclamations end with an exclamation mark.

A. Put quotation marks around each of the following sentences and capitals and punctuation marks in the proper place. On the following line, name the kind of sentence by its first letter: S, Q, C, or E.

1. where on earth have you been___________
2. heavens, you had me worried to death_____
3. don't you ever run off like that again______
4. I was afraid you had been run over________
5. why didn't you telephone me____________
6. I would have come and picked you up_____
7. listen to me when I'm talking to you_______
8. you are simply impossible_______________
9. you owe me an explanation ____________
10. good gracious, she's running away again _____

B. Put capitals, punctuation, and quotation marks in the right places in the following sentences.

1. where are you going asked the police officer
2. I'm not telling the little boy said
3. the police officer looked at him and asked what's your name
4. I won't tell you answered the boy
5. does your mother know you're out asked the officer
6. the little boy muttered no
7. don't you think she'll worry the officer said
8. she won't care said the little boy
9. here comes a lady now said the officer
10. Billy, where have you been the lady cried you had me worried sick

Give yourself 5 points for each correct sentence. Take off 2 points for each mistake. Correct your mistakes before you go on.

Chapter 8

Capital Letters

We have already discussed the major uses of capital letters: for the first word in a sentence, and for proper nouns which are the names of persons, places, or specific things, such as the *Empire State Building*. It is sometimes difficult to decide when a capital should be used. For example, *my mother,* as one of many mothers, would not be capitalized; but *Mother,* used as a name for a specific person, would be.

Example

Our family's church is The
First Baptist Church.

Here the first *church* is not capitalized because it refers to churches in general. *The First Baptist Church* is the title of a specific church; it is, therefore, capitalized.

There are other uses for capitals, chiefly in poetry and religious prose. Modern practices, however, are changing. Traditionally, every line of a poem or a hymn begins with a capital letter. Religious references to God, the Lord, the Virgin Mother, and the Holy Spirit are also capitalized. The pronouns *Thee* and *Thou* which refer to God always used to be capitalized, but that practice is changing with the modern usage of *you* and *your*.

Capitals are used for exclamations such as *Oh,* for the pronoun *I,* and for all important words in a title, including the first. They are also used for initials and for titles such as *Reverend,* which, although it may be abbreviated to *Rev.,* still retains a capital.

The following exercises will give practice in all these uses of capital letters.

Rules for Capitals

A capital is used

1. for the first word in a sentence.
2. for the first word in a line of poetry.
3. for days of the week, months, and holidays.
4. for the name of a particular person, place, or thing—in other words, a proper noun.

EXERCISE 70

Put a capital above the proper letter wherever it is needed in these sentences.

1. this is the first day of october.
2. tom and dick both live in springfield.
3. star light, star bright,

   first star I see tonight.
4. marie and ellen live in pittsburgh.
5. thank you for the book you sent me for

   christmas.

6. should old acquaintance be forgot and
   never brought to mind?
   should old acquaintance be forgot and
   days of auld lang syne?
7. columbus discovered america on october 12, 1492.
8. rick brought katie to the party.
9. there is a zoo in central park in the middle of new york city.
10. george washington lived in mt. vernon, virginia.

EXERCISE 71

Put in capitals and punctuation marks in the following sentences.

1. my birthday is on saturday, october 23
2. joe's birthday is the next day, sunday
3. joe and victor are my best friends
4. the president of the united states lives in the white house
5. roses are red, violets are blue,
   sugar is sweet and so are you
6. i love christmas even better than thanksgiving
7. columbia university is in new york city
8. dr. fisher is our family doctor
9. near us is the coliseum
10. my country, 'tis of thee,
    sweet land of liberty,
    of thee I sing

More Rules for Capitals

1. Capitals are used for *I* and *O* or *Oh.*

Example

Oh dear, I am late for work!

2. Capitals are used for words referring to God.

Example

Hear me, O Lord, when I cry unto Thee;
I will sing praises unto my God.

3. Capitals are used for the first word and for all important words in a title. Titles of books and other publications are underlined.

Example

Our English book is called Step-by-Step Guide to Correct English.

EXERCISE 72

Put capitals where needed in the following sentences.

1. o give thanks unto the lord for he is good.
2. i wish i had a new ford.
3. my father reads the daily news.
4. oh nuts, i forgot my lunch!
5. why, o why, am i so stupid?
6. the wind in the willows is a good book.

7. show me thy ways, o lord; teach me thy paths.
8. have you read the adventures of tom sawyer?
9. my composition is called the first president of the united states.
10. the lord is my shepherd; i shall not want.

Put capitals where needed in the following poem.

THE DAFFODILS

i wandered lonely as a cloud
that floats on high o'er vales and hills,
when all at once i saw a crowd,
a host of golden daffodils,
beside the lake, beneath the trees,
fluttering and dancing in the breeze.

William Wordsworth

Initials and Abbreviations

Every initial is written with a capital and is followed by a period.

Example
James Frick Sawyer—J. F. Sawyer

Most abbreviations begin with capitals and end with periods.

Example
Captain Joshua Booth—Capt. J. Booth
Doctor Daniel Berman—Dr. D. Berman

EXERCISE 73

Put capitals and periods where needed in the following sentences.

1. my name is joseph w wiley
2. i live at 3 rutland rd in great neck, n y
3. the ship is commanded by capt peter smith
4. the director of the f b i lives in washington, d c
5. gen johnson commands the armed forces of the u s a
6. i got a b s degree from city college
7. rev keating lives at 35 w fourteenth st, n y c
8. mr and mrs j williams, jr live at 19 lynn rd, springdale, mass
9. samuel schulman, m d has an office in the medical bldg
10. his office hours begin at 10 a m

EXERCISE 74

What do these initials stand for? Look in the dictionary for those you do not know.

1. P. M. ____________
2. F. B. I. ____________
3. B. C. ____________
4. A. D. ____________
5. U. N. ____________
6. P. O. ____________
7. U. S. A. ____________
8. N. Y. C. ____________
9. M. D. ____________
10. A. M. ____________

Practice in Capitals and Abbreviations

EXERCISE 75

Put capitals and periods where needed in these sentences.

1. thomas jefferson wrote the declaration of independence
2. george washington was our first president
3. abraham lincoln composed the gettysburg address
4. the battle of bunker hill began the american revolution
5. the liberty bell is in a museum in philadelphia
6. the empire state building used to be the tallest building in the world
7. radio city is at 49th st and fifth ave in new york
8. the mississippi river flows into the gulf of mexico
9. hawaii and alaska are our newest states
10. children believe santa claus lives at the north pole

EXERCISE 76

Write the abbreviations for

1. Street ____________________
2. Road ____________________
3. January ____________________
4. December ____________________
5. Monday ____________________
6. Tuesday ____________________
7. Wednesday ____________________
8. October ____________________
9. Nebraska ____________________
10. Connecticut ____________________
11. Thursday ____________________
12. February ____________________
13. Massachusetts ____________________
14. Friday ____________________
15. November ____________________
16. Mountain ____________________
17. Doctor ____________________
18. Professor ____________________
19. Saturday ____________________
20. General ____________________

Review of Capitals

Capitals are used for

1. the first word in a sentence.
2. the first word in a line of poetry.
3. days of the week, months, and holidays.
4. the name of a particular person, place, or thing.

5. *I* and *O* or *Oh.*

6. words referring to God.

7. initials.

8. the important words in titles.

9. most abbreviations.

Review Test of Capitals

EXERCISE 77

A. Put capitals and periods wherever needed in the following sentences.

1. george, elvis, and john have a rock group, the weirdos
2. thanksgiving day comes on november 22 this year
3. dr anderson lives in mt hermon, mass
4. hear me, oh lord, when i pray unto thee
5. julie's father is in the f b i
6. prof dennis teaches at columbia university
7. the name of my book is a tale of two cities
8. saturday is my favorite day of the week
9. i will send your package c o d to 231 main st, springfield, mass
10. sing a song of seasons,

    something bright in all,

    flowers in the summer,

    fires in the fall!

B. Punctuate the following sentences. Put capitals where needed.

1. where are you going asked my brother
2. out to play baseball i answered
3. he shouted after me hey, can i come
4. oh i guess so i said
5. we headed down main street toward prospect park
6. dr j f robbins works at the dallas city hospital
7. corp g steward lives at 10 main st denver col
8. judy said she would be home by 12 p m
9. she didn't come until 2 a m
10. boys flying kites haul in their white-winged birds

    you can't do that way when you're flying words

    thoughts unexpressed may sometimes fall back dead

    but god himself can't change them once they're said

    Will Carlton

Give yourself 5 points for each correct sentence. Take off 1 point for each mistake. Be sure you understand why you made errors.

Chapter 9

Adjectives

Adjectives are words that *describe* nouns or pronouns. These are the words that give life and color and fill out the bare bones of a sentence. Notice the difference that adjectives make in the two sentences below.

Examples

The guard approached the prisoner.

The huge, powerful, angry guard approached the frightened, cowering prisoner.

The words *huge*, *powerful*, and *angry* all describe the guard menacingly approaching the *frightened*, *cowering* prisoner.

Adjectives are usually found just before the noun that they *describe* or *modify*, although sometimes they follow it as in this sentence:

Example

The prisoner, frightened and cowering, shrank into the corner of his cell.

Often adjectives follow a verb of being; and, although they are then part of the predicate, they describe the subject. These are called *predicate adjectives*.

Examples

I am hungry.

Her dress was elegant.

Most adjectives have three forms which are used in comparing qualities.

Example

Jim is tall. (*Tall* describes Jim, even though it is in the predicate.)

Joe is taller than Jim. (There must be two of anything in order to compare them.)

Harry is the tallest. (There must be three or more to compare before this form can be used.)

Most adjectives can be compared simply by adding *er* or *est*. The rest can be compared by adding the words *more* or *most* in front of them.

Example

Sally is beautiful.

Nina is more beautiful.

But Joanna is the most beautiful girl I know.

There are also a few irregular adjectives which change in form as they are compared. Some examples are *good*, *better*, and *best*. These you will have to memorize.

Some adjectives cannot be compared because they are already "the most." Words like *perfect* or *empty* cannot be compared. If a thing is perfect, how can it be more perfect? *Unique* is another such word. If there is only one such thing in the world, then there is nothing to be compared with it.

Last of all, there are a number of little words which do not seem to describe very much but, in fact, act as adjectives. These are words such as *each*, *which*, *my*, *some*, and *what*. Along with them we will group *the*, *a*, and *an*, the words called articles. As we have already seen (p. 19), they refer to specific or nonspecific nouns. All of these words add meaning and clarity to the sentence in which they are used.

Descriptive Adjectives

EXERCISE 78

An *adjective* is a word that describes a noun, giving it color and meaning. It is usually found just before the noun it *describes* or *modifies*.

Diagram these sentences and circle the descriptive adjectives. There are at least thirty adjectives. Can you find them?

Example
The (fat) (red) hen / waddled across the (dusty) yard.

1. The slim, long-haired girl waited on a busy corner.
2. She wore a pink shirt and ragged blue jeans.
3. My new car has bucket seats and red upholstery.
4. The big brown dog chased the frightened thief.
5. The brightest girl on our block is little Beth.
6. The big black cat sat in the sunny window of the grocery store.
7. On cold winter nights I like a blazing fire.
8. The icy wind blows stinging snow down the narrow streets.
9. But in our cheerful kitchen is a warm stove.
10. His plump rosy mother hums an old Italian song while she cooks delicious lasagna.

EXERCISE 79

Fill the spaces below with adjectives to describe the nouns in the sentences.

1. The _________ girls giggled as the _________ boys walked by.
2. A _________ skyscraper is being built overlooking the _________ bay.
3. A _________ breeze blew in from the _________ ocean.
4. He drove his _________ convertible down the _________ highway.
5. A _________ basket of flowers stood on the _________ table.
6. A _________ girl rode on the _________ bicycle.
7. The _________ boy was eating _________ ice cream with _________ sauce.
8. In my grandmother's _________ house I could smell a _________ pie baking.
9. On Monday morning the woman wore a _________ blouse and a _________ skirt.
10. She had _________ shoes and a _________ pocketbook.

Predicate Adjectives

EXERCISE 80

An adjective often precedes the noun it modifies. But sometimes an adjective is found in the predicate after a verb of being. It is called a *predicate adjective* if it modifies the subject, which may be a noun or a pronoun.

Examples
I / am happy. The barn / is red.

In these examples *happy* describes how I am, and the adjective *red* describes the barn just as much as if the phrase "the red barn" had been used instead.

Diagram the following sentences and draw an arrow to connect the predicate adjective with the subject it modifies.

1. My house is green.
2. The supper was delicious.
3. The boys were noisy.
4. Your picture is beautiful.
5. The weather was hot.
6. But the evenings were cool.
7. I am busy this week.
8. That school is big.
9. My boss is strict.
10. But she is fair.

EXERCISE 81

In the following sentences both ordinary adjectives and predicate adjectives will be found. Diagram the sentences and connect each adjective with an arrow to the noun or pronoun it modifies.

1. My house is white with green shutters.
2. My rattly old car was blue.
3. His new convertible is red with a black top.
4. The cool cotton dress is blue and white.
5. The young people were happy and noisy.
6. I am sad and lonely tonight.
7. We are crowded in our small apartment.
8. The park is lovely in the warm spring weather.
9. The busy highway is full of speeding cars.
10. The giant plane is high over the gray storm clouds.

Comparing Adjectives

EXERCISE 82

An *adjective* is a word that describes a noun or a pronoun. When you wish to compare two nouns, you change the form of the adjective, usually by adding *er*.

Examples
John is tall.
Ricky is taller than John.
Which apple is smaller (of the two apples)?

If you are comparing three or more nouns, add *est* to the adjective.

Examples
Judy is the brightest student in the class.
Tom is the shortest boy on the team.

After each of the following sentences, state how many nouns are being compared: two, or three, or more.

Examples

My car is faster than yours. (Compares two cars. Write 2.)

I have the strictest teacher in the school. (Compares three or more teachers. Write 3+.)

1. I am taller than my brother. _____
2. My father is the tallest in the family. _____
3. You are the nicest person I know. _____
4. My brother is much older than I. _____
5. She has the cutest baby I ever saw! _____
6. Selma and Judy are both pretty but Judy is prettier than Selma. _____
7. A quarter is larger than a dime.__________
8. Tokyo is the largest city in the world._____
9. My sister is the best lawyer in town. _____
10. The World Trade Center is higher than the Empire State Building.________________

EXERCISE 83

Compare the adjectives listed below by adding *er* or *est*. If the adjective already ends in e, add *r* or *st*. If the adjective ends in *y*, change the *y* to *i* before adding *er* or *est*.

Example

ADJECTIVE	MORE	MOST
small	smaller	smallest

1. great ____________ ____________
2. gentle ____________ ____________
3. high ____________ ____________
4. lovely ____________ ____________
5. smart ____________ ____________
6. funny ____________ ____________
7. blue ____________ ____________
8. pale ____________ ____________
9. tiny ____________ ____________
10. tame ____________ ____________

Irregular Adjectives

There are a number of words which do not seem to describe very much but act, in fact, as adjectives. Typical of these are *my*, *his*, *your*, *some*, *few*, *these*, *that*, and *hers*.

Examples

Some time	Which hat	Few people
That boy	These days	My mother
Each year	Many months	Every week

EXERCISE 84

The words *the*, *a*, and *an* act as adjectives, too. The word *the* refers to a specific noun. "Put *the* book on *the* table," refers to a specific book and a specific table. "Get me *a* book," refers to any book, not a particular one.

The word *a* is used before words beginning with *consonants* (hard sounds, such as *b*, *d*, *t*, *k*). The word *an* is used before words beginning with *vowels* (*a*, *e*, *i*, *o*, *u*,) because it sounds better to have vowel sounds separated by the consonant *n*, as in "an egg" or "an umbrella." *An* is also used before words beginning with a silent *h*, as in *honest*.

Examples

A man   An honest man

Before each of the nouns below, write *a* or *an*, depending upon whether the following word begins with a vowel, a consonant, or a silent *h*.

1. ____________ tree

2. ____________ apple

3. ____________ table

4. ____________ ocean

5. ____________ elevator

6. ____________ pencil

7. ____________ automobile

8. ____________ honor

9. ____________ lamp

10. ____________ Indian

Some adjectives are irregular and use different words to express *more* or *the most* instead of adding *er* and *est.* Here are a few of the most common ones which should be memorized.

ADJECTIVE	MORE	MOST
good, well	better	best
bad	worse	worst
little	less	least
much, many	more	most
far	further	furthest

EXERCISE 85

In the following sentences, draw arrows from all adjectives, including *the* and *a* or *an*, to the nouns or pronouns they modify.

Example
The old farmer was tired.

1. The apples from his farm are best.
2. She wore a little red bow in her blond hair.
3. I hope you are better today.
4. You are a bad dancer but your sister is worse.
5. The ice cream vendor pushed his little cart.
6. We had delicious beef, fried potatoes, and green beans.
7. It is a good thing you have an old uncle with that much energy.
8. The TV in the next apartment makes a terrible noise.
9. I want an honest answer to my last question.
10. An eagle is faster than most birds.

Review Test of Adjectives

EXERCISE 86

A. Fill in the following blanks.

1. An adjective describes a ____________ or a ____________.
2. A predicate adjective modifies or describes the ____________ of the sentence.
3. *A* is an indefinite adjective used before words beginning with a ____________.
4. *An* is an indefinite adjective used before words beginning with a ____________.

B. Diagram the following sentences. Draw arrows from each adjective to the noun or pronoun it describes.

1. The big black dog followed the tall man.
2. A white fluffy kitten sat on the front stoop.
3. My old grandmother is deaf.
4. But she is a marvelous cook.
5. In the pouring rain he ran home.
6. He had forgotten an umbrella.

7. My younger son is now taller than I am!.

8. Few people are smarter than you are.

9. That boy is the fastest runner on the track team.

10. My wife knows which desserts I like.

C. Compare the following:

ADJECTIVE	MORE	MOST
1. funny	__________	__________
2. good	__________	__________
3. red	__________	__________
4. cute	__________	__________
5. bad	__________	__________
6. silly	__________	__________
7. much	__________	__________
8. fast	__________	__________
9. lovely	__________	__________
10. wise	__________	__________

Give yourself 10 points for A, 80 points for B, and 10 points for C. Take off 1 point for each mistake. Be sure to memorize the correct form of any adjectives on which you made mistakes.

Chapter 10

Adverbs

Just as we have adjectives which describe or modify nouns, we also have *adverbs* which describe or modify *verbs*.

Example

The great ship sailed *slowly* out to sea.

The adverb *slowly* tells you *how* the ship sailed, just as the adjective *great* tells you more about the ship.

Adverbs are words that tell you how, when, where, or to what degree the action of the verb takes place.

Examples

The postman got up *early*. (Tells *when* he got up.)
He started *quickly* on his rounds. (Tells *how* he started out.)
He walked *away* from the post office. (Tells *where* he walked.)
She tried hard to win. (Tells *to what degree* she tried.)

Most adverbs are formed by adding *ly* to an adjective. If the adjective ends in *y*, as in *pretty*, the *y* is changed to *i* before the *ly* is added.

Examples

ADJECTIVE	ADVERB
slow	slowly
pretty	prettily
quiet	quietly
careful	carefully

Adverbs Formed from Adjectives

EXERCISE 87

Turn the adjectives below into adverbs by adding *ly*. Remember if the adjective ends with *y*, it should be changed to *i* before adding *ly*.

ADJECTIVE	ADVERB
1. loud	____________
2. bright	____________
3. high	____________
4. easy	____________
5. final	____________
6. silent	____________
7. usual	____________
8. close	____________
9. happy	____________
10. real	____________

EXERCISE 88

Diagram the following sentences and then circle as many adverbs as you can find.

Example
The man / walked (quickly.)

1. The carpenter hammered noisily. _________
2. The child sang happily. _________
3. The old lady spoke quietly. _________
4. The priest listened silently. _________
5. The woman wept sadly. _________
6. The mother smiled tenderly. _________
7. The baby played busily. _________
8. The dog barked loudly. _________
9. My teacher talks clearly. _________
10. The child rubbed his eyes sleepily. _________

Now go back and write beside each adverb the adjective from which it was formed.

Example
quickly quick

EXERCISE 89

Diagram the sentences below. Circle the adverb in each one. Write the adjective from which it was formed beside it.

1. A man whistled cheerfully. _________
2. The sun shone brightly. _________
3. A girl sang softly to herself. _________
4. The black cat purred contentedly. _________
5. The radio blared loudly on the porch. _____
6. The train roared noisily away. _________
7. A man skated rapidly across the pond. _____
8. The driver shouted angrily at his son. _____
9. The powerful car roared swiftly down the highway. _________
10. The boat drifted lazily on the calm sea. _____

Irregular Adverbs

EXERCISE 90

Not all adverbs are formed by adding *ly* to an adjective. Words such as *always, well, often, away,* and *far* are also adverbs because they tell you something about the verb. An adverb may follow or come before the verb it modifies.

Example
He (always) sits in that chair.

Always describes the verb *sits.* It tells you *when* the action of the verb takes place. Remember that adverbs usually answer *how, where,* or *when.*

Diagram each of the following sentences. Then circle the adverb and in the space provided write which of the three questions above it answers about the verb.

Example
The boy / plays the piano (well.) *How?*

1. The thief ran fast. _________
2. My son always gets speeding tickets. _____
3. I often run out of money. _________
4. The police went away at last. _________

5. The truck driver ate greedily.____________

6. Tony does well at his job.______________

7. My boyfriend left early.______________

8. He answered quickly when I called.________

9. I see better with glasses.________________

10. He traveled far from home.____________

EXERCISE 91

In the sentences below, adjectives have been used incorrectly to describe the action of the verbs. Find one in each sentence and turn it into an adverb by adding *ly*.

1. The poor widow wept silent.
2. The noisy boys yell loud.
3. The men were working quiet.
4. Slow the moon rose in the east.
5. The stars shine bright in the sky.
6. He leaped light over the rocks.
7. The man spoke sad to his priest.
8. The doctor worked quick to dress the cut.
9. He has been exercising regular.
10. The mother spoke loving to the child.

Verb Modifiers

EXERCISE 92

The word *not* is a little adverb that modifies the verb by reversing its meaning.

Example

Chuck did *not* come home.

Not tells how Chuck came home.

Circle all the adverbs you find in the following sentences and draw arrows to the verbs they modify. There are 12 of them. After you locate them, read the sentences again and notice what they add to their meanings.

1. My friend spoke softly to me.
2. The workers laughed merrily at the joke.
3. You have not finished your work.
4. The boy crept cautiously up the stairs.
5. They moved creakily under his weight.
6. I wish you would listen carefully to me.
7. I felt better after I took the medicine.
8. He did not like to go far from home.
9. We always eat dinner at six o'clock.
10. I often leave the office late.

EXERCISE 93

Circle all the adverbs you find in the following sentences and draw arrows to the verbs they modify.

1. The thief crept silently down the hall.
2. The phone on the table rang loudly.
3. He jumped nervously at the sound.
4. She comes frequently to my house.
5. I do not always see you in church.
6. Please do not yell loudly in the house.

7. They often take trips to the beach.

8. Al never told me about that.

9. He does not talk about other people.

10. But he always listens to them.

Comparing Adverbs

Adverbs modify verbs; they also modify other adverbs.

Example

He spoke *very* carefully.

Carefully is an adverb telling you *how* the subject spoke; *very* is an adverb modifying the adverb *carefully*.

EXERCISE 94

In the following sentences draw arrows to indicate what each adverb modifies.

Example

The dog barked very loudly.

1. The boy studied so hard for his exam.

2. She worked very carefully at her knitting.

3. Please come in more quietly.

4. She sang so sweetly that the baby stopped crying.

5. He shouted very loudly for help.

6. She criticizes more quickly than I.

7. Jack works much harder than you do.

8. I feel very well, thank you.

9. The lady spoke most kindly to him.

10. Please do not go so far from home.

An adverb can be compared by putting *more*/*less* or *most*/*least* before it.

Examples

Jim studies *more* carefully than Dick.
Mary tried *most* willingly to help me.
He drove *less* rapidly on the mountain roads.

EXERCISE 95

There are two adverbs after each sentence. Choose the appropriate one to fill in the space in each sentence. Notice how your choice changes the meaning of the other adverb it modifies.

1. John drove ___________ carefully after his accident. (more, less)

2. Mary is ___________ dependable than Jean, who is disorganized. (more, less)

3. She works __________ efficiently. (most, least)

4. Please come in __________ noisily. (more, less)

5. Jim spoke __________ rudely after I had explained things to him. (less, more)

6. She answered me ____________ graciously. (most, least)

7. The doctor operated ___________ efficiently with good lighting. (more, less)

8. His old car travels ___________ rapidly than mine. (more, less)

9. She solved the problem ___________ intelligently. (most, least)

10. She works __________ effectively when she is tired. (less, more)

Troublemakers: Good and Well

Good is an adjective and describes a noun.

Example

Mac does *good* work.

Well is an adverb and describes a verb.

Example

Mac works *well.*

Exception: *Well* is used as an adjective when referring to a person's health.

Example

How is your mother? She is *well,* thank you.

In this case, *good* and *well* do not mean the same thing. A good mother is not the same as a well mother. *Well* describes how she feels, her state of being.

EXERCISE 96

In the following sentences, fill in *good* or *well* in the blanks, depending on whether you are describing a noun or a verb.

1. Beth always behaves herself; she is a _______ girl.
2. Beth always behaves herself____________.
3. John learned his lesson______________.
4. He got a_____________mark on the test.
5. A_____________man is sometimes called a saint.
6. Nancy did her job______________.
7. That is a_____________book.
8. Jimmy's work in the shop is____________.
9. Eddie repairs cars very______________.
10. I feel very_____________, thank you.

EXERCISE 97

In the following sentences using *good* and *well,* cross out the incorrect word and write in the proper one in the space provided.

Example

Jim studies ~~good.~~ *well*

1. Theresa did good in school today.________
2. Why don't you behave good?____________
3. You didn't paint good today.____________
4. He did his work goodly.________________
5. Congratulations! You spoke good in the meeting. ____________________________
6. You learned your lesson good.___________
7. Jim did a well job.___________________
8. Jenny served the guests goodly.__________
9. Miss Johnson told a well story.__________
10. Ted shoots a well game of pool. _________

Adjective Modifiers

Adverbs modify verbs and other adverbs; they also modify adjectives. Adverbs tell *how, when, where,* or *to what degree.*

Example

Ralph is a very good mechanic.

Good is an adjective describing mechanic. *Very* is an adverb that tells *to what degree* Ralph is good.

Some adjectives are not compared by adding *er* and *est*. In such a case, the adverbs *more* and *most* are used with the adjectives in referring to two, or to more than two, comparisons.

pretty	prettier	prettiest
beautiful	more beautiful	most beautiful

Example

Jean is *more* reliable than her sister.
She is the *most* reliable person in the class.

Diagram the following sentences. From each adverb draw an arrow to the adjective it modifies.

Example

I / am so tired.

EXERCISE 98

1. A very big dog barked at me.
2. Jimmy was always hungry.
3. May grew terribly fat.
4. My legs are always tired!
5. She looked more pleased than ever.
6. The boy grew extremely tall.
7. We are most happy about this.
8. Ted ran very fast up the hill.
9. The stranger came from a most distant land.
10. Patty was so friendly today!

EXERCISE 99

Compare the following adjectives, either by adding *er* and *est* or by putting *more* or *most* before them. Note that some words may be formed either way.

weak __________ __________

patient __________ __________

kind __________ __________

delicious __________ __________

tight __________ __________

happy __________ __________

fragrant __________ __________

miserable __________ __________

pleasant __________ __________

careful __________ __________

Review of Adverbs and Adjectives

Adverbs modify verbs, adjectives, and other adverbs. They answer the questions *how, when, where,* and *to what degree.*

In the following sentences, show with an arrow what word each adverb modifies. After each sentence, tell what question the adverb answers.

Example

The boy is very tall. *To what degree*?

EXERCISE 100

1. Teddy runs fast. __________
2. The child cried often. __________
3. The old man walked slowly. __________
4. The door slammed suddenly. __________
5. Her phone rang immediately. __________

6. I am very hungry. ____________________

7. My grandfather got too tired. ____________

8. The little girl is just three. ______________

9. Every day Tim grew more lonely. _________

10. The children are most excited! ___________

EXERCISE 101

Adjectives modify nouns and pronouns. Adverbs modify verbs, adjectives, and other adverbs. In each sentence below, choose between the adjective and the adverb by deciding what word is being modified. Underline the correct choice.

Example
Jimmy does (careful, carefully) work.

The noun *work* is being described. Since an adjective is needed to describe a noun, the adjective *careful* is the correct choice.

Example
Jimmy works (careful, carefully).

In this sentence, the verb *works* is being modified. Therefore, the adverb *carefully* is needed.

1. The manager spoke in a (quiet, quietly) voice.

2. Joe answered him (polite, politely).

3. He comes (regular, regularly) to my house.

4. The bull was big and (strong, strongly).

5. Janie plays the guitar (good, well).

6. Davie ate his lunch (quick, quickly).

7. His wife made him a (quick, quickly) lunch.

8. I am a (slow, slowly) thinker.

9. I think very (slow, slowly).

10. Julie's embroidery is (beautiful, beautifully).

More Troublemakers

Too—an adverb with two meanings. When followed by a describing adjective or adverb, it means *too much* of anything. When set off by a comma, it means *also*.

Examples
too fat, too thin, too cold, too hastily
I want to play, too (also).

To—to do something. It is part of a verb form. It also expresses direction.

Examples
to run, to jump, to shout
to go to the station

Two—the number 2, an adjective that tells how many.

EXERCISE 102

Put the proper word (too, to, or two) in each blank space.

1. I am going _________ the park.

2. I want _________ go, _________.

3. The _________ of us will go.

4. We want _________ go _________ church.

5. It is _________ hot _________ work.

6. I have _________ sisters, _________.

7. It's _________ much trouble _________ do it.

8. This is__________ hard __________read.

9. She's__________ busy __________talk.

10. The apple is__________ green __________ eat.

There—an adverb meaning "in that place"; also used in sentences which start "There is" or "There are."
Their—an adjective meaning "belonging to them"; it is always followed by a noun.

Example
There is someone in there.
He is in their house.

EXERCISE 103

Put the proper word (there, their) in each blank space in these sentences.

1. __________is too much noise in__________ room.

2. __________office is over__________.

3. She is in__________club, too.

4. __________were twenty people on__________ bus.

5. __________house is too far away; we can't walk__________.

6. __________is something I don't understand about__________behavior.

7. __________ are the men I told you about; they are over__________ .

8. I left my book on the table over__________.

9. __________are too many people who want __________own way.

10. __________is no reason for__________ critical attitude in this matter.

EXERCISE 104

Use each of the following phrases correctly in a sentence on the line below it.

Example
was there
The teacher was there.

there is

____

too much

____

over there

____

their wishes

____

there are

____

to go there

____

too many

____

to church

____

went there

____

their customs

____

too hot to work

____

their names

____

Review Test of Adjectives and Adverbs

EXERCISE 105

A. An adjective modifies a____________or a __________. An adverb modifies a__________, an___________, or another___________. Adverbs answer the questions ________, ________, ________, and ________ ________ ________.

B. After each of the following words, write *adj.* or *adv.* to indicate which each one is.

kind	__________	handsome	__________
gently	__________	funny	__________
rapid	__________	lately	__________
green	__________	pretty	__________
rapidly	__________	often	__________
beautiful	__________	very	__________
good	__________	weak	__________
well	__________		

C. Diagram each of the following sentences. Draw arrows from each adverb to the verb, adjective, or adverb it modifies.

Example

The taxi / honked (loudly) in the street.

1. Dulcie walked slowly home from work.
2. She was not very happy.
3. The boss was terribly mean to her.
4. Her mother called loudly from the window.
5. She was almost late for supper.
6. She did not feel very hungry.
7. Dulcie was often lonely.
8. But tonight she felt more lonely than usual.
9. Then the telephone rang suddenly.
10. Dulcie had a very nice surprise!

D. In each of the following, tell whether the adverb underlined modifies a verb, an adjective, or another adverb.

Example

too tired *adj.*

1. very slowly____________________
2. so heavy____________________
3. worked hard ____________________
4. slept restlessly ____________________
5. much later ____________________
6. most wonderful____________________
7. so delightfully____________________
8. too heavily____________________
9. studied well ____________________
10. too hard ____________________

E. After each adverb tell what question it answers: *how, when, where,* or *to what degree.*

rapidly	__________	lovingly	__________
daily	__________	often	__________
more	__________	away	__________
lately	__________	so	__________
nearby	__________	sometimes	__________

Give yourself 3 points for each sentence in C and 2 points for all the other questions you answer correctly. Do not count A. Take off 2 points for each mistake. How well did you do? Be sure to review your mistakes before going on.

Chapter 11

More Punctuation

We have already been introduced to commas, periods, and quotation marks. We have learned that a comma is used to indicate a pause and that it can change the whole meaning of a sentence.

Examples

Don hit him.
Don, hit him!

In the second sentence, *Don* is a noun of address, which means any name someone is called. It could be a proper name like *Don,* or it could be a term of endearment, such as *dear* or *honey.* It could also be a teasing or insulting name, such as *stupid* or *dummy.*

Example

Look, idiot, you ought to be fired!

Here the word *idiot* is used as a noun of address and is set off from the rest of the sentence by commas before and after it.

Another use for commas is to set off a noun which follows another noun and describes it in some way. Such a noun is said to be *in apposition to* the noun it describes.

Example

Tony, my brother, hit a home run.

Here the commas before and after *my brother* indicate that Tony is the brother spoken of. The two commas are very important. If the second one is left out, the sentence reads:

Tony, my brother hit a home run.

This sounds as if Tony were a noun of address and that the speaker is telling Tony about the home run of another person, his brother.

Another use for commas is to indicate pauses in a series of three or more words. A series of two words requires no pause; "the fat red hen" needs no comma. But a long phrase such as "the sleek, black, elegant cat" requires two commas or one less than the number of words in the series. There is no pause between the words *elegant* and *cat.* If the sentence were turned around to read "The cat was sleek, black, and elegant," there would still be two commas after the first two of the three adjectives. There must be at least three words in a series; they must all be the same kind of words (nouns, adjectives, etc.); and there is always one comma less than there are words in the series.

These are a few of the six rules for the use of commas which you can practice in the following exercises. The rest are fairly simple or have already been introduced: for example, the use of commas to set off quotations from the rest of the sentence (review page 78).

Rules for Commas

Commas are used wherever a pause is required.

Examples

After turning off the TV, Mary went to bed.
Running to the door, he slammed it shut.

There are six common rules for using commas. Learn each one. Then put commas where they belong in the practice sentences.

RULE 1

Commas are used to separate parts of an address or a date.

Example

I live at 4 Beach Drive, Santa Monica, California.
It happened on Sunday, April 22, 1975.

EXERCISE 106

1. My birthday was last Tuesday September 9th.
2. I come from Greenfield Mass.
3. I was born on June 30 1962.
4. My grandmother lives at 4 Locust Lane Springfield.
5. Do you mean Springfield Massachusetts or Springfield Illinois?
6. Valentine's Day is on Tuesday February 14.
7. I'll be at the Hilton Hotel Los Angeles California.
8. You can reach me there until Wednesday March 18.
9. I'll be back home on Friday night March 20.
10. My address is 16 Ridge Road Arlington Virginia.

RULE 2

Words like *Oh, yes, no, well,* and *however* are set off from the rest of the sentence by commas.

Example

Oh, well, I don't care.

EXERCISE 107

1. Well shall we get started?
2. Yes it's about time we did.
3. I'm afraid however that we will be late.
4. Oh no I don't agree with you!
5. Well we shall see who is right.
6. You may however be surprised by what happens!
7. No I don't think so.
8. Well I could be wrong I suppose.
9. Yes you certainly could!
10. Oh well we'll soon find out who's right.

RULE 3

A noun of address is a name used in speaking to someone. It is set off by a comma from the rest of the sentence if it is at the beginning or end of the sentence. If it is in the middle of the sentence, it is set off by two commas, one before it and one after it.

Examples

Is that you, Ed?
Donna, your telephone is ringing.
Listen, Harry, I told you to forget it!

EXERCISE 108

1. Joe please close the door.________________

2. I asked you Joe to close the door.__________
3. Honey do you like this dress on me?______
4. Are you listening to me Peter?__________
5. Please get some ice Julie and bring it out here.________________
6. Sheila would you write that letter for me?__
7. Watch out Jim he'll bite you!____________
8. I warned you Phil to keep your dog tied up. ______________
9. Darling where on earth have you been?____
10. I've been waiting for you dear for an hour! ______________

Do you remember the four kinds of sentences? In the spaces above, write what kind of sentence each one is. If you have forgotten, refer back to Chapter 5, page 45.

RULE 4

Words in a series of three or more are separated by commas. There is always one less comma than there are words in a series.

Example
My brothers are Charlie, Sandy, and Ray.

EXERCISE 109

1. Our flag is red white and blue.
2. Today we have fried chicken shrimps and spareribs.
3. My favorite sports are skating soccer and basketball.
4. The big brown hungry bear headed for the campfire.
5. Dave Ed and Joe took off hastily when they saw him.
6. The lady was hot tired and cross.
7. She had been to department stores specialty stores and discount stores.
8. She had been jostled bumped and pushed around.
9. Now all she wanted was rest peace and quiet.
10. Instead she found her children quarreling crying and fighting each other.

RULE 5

A noun next to another noun is said to be *in apposition* to it and is called an *appositive*. An *appositive* explains the first noun in some way and is set off by commas.

Example
Mr. Jones, the chairman, called the meeting to order.

EXERCISE 110

Punctuate the following sentences.

1. Millie my sister has a new dress.
2. Elizabeth II the Queen of England has four children.
3. Miss Cass I want you to meet my mother Mrs. Salerno.
4. This is my friend Ed Mahoney.
5. The lawyer Mr. Williams called us to his office.

6. Our minister Rev. Parker preached a fine sermon.

7. My father Jack Grillo is a taxi driver.

8. The captain of the baseball team Joe Murray is my pal.

9. The tiger a dangerous animal does not make a good pet.

10. Paul Tribuno the winner of the match made a short speech.

RULE 6

Commas are used to set off quotations from the rest of the sentence, except where the quotation ends in an exclamation or a question mark.

Example
"Once upon a time," began the grandmother, "there were three bears."

EXERCISE 111

In the following sentences, put in commas and quotation marks.

1. Jimmy where are you? cried the mother.

2. Jimmy she cried where are you?

3. Come here called the boss.

4. The boss called Come here!

5. Where is Kent Place? the confused driver asked.

6. Can you tell me asked the driver where Kent Place is?

7. Turn left at the next corner the policeman said. It's the first street on your right.

8. You can't miss it he added. There's a mailbox on the corner.

9. Thanks, officer said the driver for helping me out.

10. Don't mention it he replied. I'm glad to help.

Review of Commas

Commas indicate a pause and are used

1. to separate parts of addresses and dates.
2. to set off words like *yes, no,* and *however.*
3. to set off nouns of address.
4. to separate words in a series.
5. to set off appositives.
6. to set off quotations.

EXERCISE 112

Punctuate the following sentences. Whenever you use a comma, place above it the number of the rule which you are applying.

Example
6
My mother called , "Come here, Janie."

1. Our grandmother's birthday is next Saturday February 23

2. Grandmother how old will you be then asked Tony

3. We're having a party at her home at 129 14th Street Cleveland Ohio

4. My mother Mrs. Salerno has made a big cake

5. My cousins Tony Joe Douglas and Mike are all invited

6. Joe however will not be able to come

7. Joe I hope you are coming to the party said my mother

8. No I can't said Joe I have to go to the dentist

9. Well come afterwards suggested Tony

10. Yes I could do that said Joe Thanks a lot Tony

Review Test of Punctuation

EXERCISE 113

Put capitals and punctuation in the following sentences.

1. waitress can I have the meat loaf special asked eddie

2. it's all gone but we have stew corned beef and fried fish said the waitress

3. oh nuts said eddie i just feel like having meat loaf

4. well said the waitress how about a hamburger

5. no i had one for lunch said eddie

6. look waitress does the stew have dumplings he asked

7. yes i think so she answered

8. ok i'll try that said eddie

9. here you are said the waitress i hope you like it

10. thank you it hits the spot said eddie

Take off 1 point for every error. How did you do? If you have over 80 on this test, you have a good working knowledge of proper punctuation. Review your mistakes before going on to the next chapter.

Chapter 12

Prepositions

A preposition is a little word used with a noun to tell what, when, where, or how.

Example

The men walked on the moon.

The phrase *on the moon* tells *where* the men walked. It is not a sentence because it does not express a complete thought; it has no subject and no predicate. It is simply a group of words, called a *phrase*, which contributes more information. When the phrase begins with a preposition, it is called a *prepositional phrase.*

Pre is Latin for *before* and a *preposition* is *in a position before* the noun which is its object. Previously we have discussed objects of the verb (see Chapter 2). You will recall that these are direct objects which receive the action of the verb.

Example

Al threw the baseball.

Here, *the baseball* is the direct object which is thrown.

Example

Al threw the baseball to Dave.

Here the prepositional phrase *to Dave* tells *where* Al threw the baseball.

Indirect Objects

Sometimes we leave out the word *to*. Then it becomes implied in the sentence.

Example

Al threw (to) Dave the baseball.

In this case, where the preposition *to* is left out, there is no prepositional phrase. The noun *Dave* becomes the *indirect object* of the verb. The direct object is the baseball which received the action of throwing. The indirect object is Dave, to whom the ball is thrown.

There are many sentences like this in English. Often a pronoun is used as an indirect object.

Examples

Al threw him the baseball.
Her husband gave her some money.

To help you locate the indirect object, see if the preposition *to*, or sometimes *for*, would make sense in front of it.

Example

The traffic cop gave (to) the driver a ticket.
The delivery man left (for) me a package.

EXERCISE 114

Read the following sentences and underline the

indirect object in each one. It may be a noun or a pronoun. Check your work by saying "to" or "for" before each indirect object to see if it makes sense.

1. I handed Henry the letter.

2. She gave the baby his bottle.

3. The secretary took her boss the mail.

4. The man left the waiter a tip.

5. Joe got his son a new bike.

6. He gave him the bike for his birthday.

7. Will you please pass me some coffee?

8. The live wire gave him a bad shock.

9. Mrs. Gibbs told Mrs. Murphy the latest gossip.

10. I gave Mr. Kirby your message.

Now go back and circle the direct objects which receive the action of the verb.

Common Prepositions

There are many prepositions which, when combined with a noun, form prepositional phrases which explain *what*, *when*, *where*, and *how*. The noun is called the *object of the preposition.*

Examples

(what) (where)
A flock *of sheep* graze *in the meadow.*

(when) (how)
After his lunch he worked *like a beaver.*

The most common prepositions are listed below.

at	down
by	from
in	into
of	like
off	over
on	past
to	upon
up	with
for	about
above	below
across	beside
after	between
against	during
along	except
among	through
around	toward
before	underneath
behind	without

EXERCISE 115

Diagram the following sentences. In each one, circle the prepositional phrase.

Example

The boy / sat (on the porch.)

1. Marie and Debbie ran up the steps.

2. They put their books on the table.

3. He took a box from the shelf.

4. Her sister came down the stairs.

5. She invited them into the living room.

6. They sat down on the couch.

7. We looked at a new book.

8. Later they went to the movies.

9. The toys were left on the floor.

10. She carried the dishes to the kitchen.

EXERCISE 116

For each of the phrases you circled in Exercise

115, write the little preposition and the noun which is its object in the columns below.

Example

The boy sat (on the porch.)

PREPOSITION	OBJECT
on	porch
1. ______	______
2. ______	______
3. ______	______
4. ______	______
5. ______	______
6. ______	______
7. ______	______
8. ______	______
9. ______	______
10. ______	______

Prepositional Phrases

The different kinds of words used in our language are called *parts of speech.* We have now learned six parts of speech. Let us review them.

Part of Speech	DEFINITION
Noun	A person, place, or thing
Pronoun	Stands in place of a noun
Adjective	Describes a noun or a pronoun
Verb	Supplies the action or being in a sentence
Adverb	Describes a verb, adjective, or another adverb
Preposition	A little word with a noun as its object

A prepositional phrase is often used instead of an adjective to describe a noun. In this case it is called an *adjective phrase.*

Example

A silk dress (*silk* is an adjective)

A dress of silk (*of silk* is a prepositional phrase used as an adjective to describe the noun *dress*)

EXERCISE 117

Make up sentences using the following groups of words. These contain adjective phrases which describe nouns. Write your sentences on the line below.

1. A flock of sheep

____

____

2. A cap with a feather

____

____

3. A man in uniform

____

____

4. Materials for writing

____

____

5. A prince of royal blood

____

____

In each sentence you have written, circle the prepositional phrase and draw an arrow to the noun it describes or modifies. These are all adjective phrases.

Example

She wore a dress (of silk.)

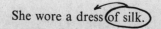

A prepositional phrase is often used instead of an adverb to modify a verb, an adjective, or another adverb. This is called an *adverb phrase.*

Example

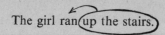

The girl ran up the stairs.

Up the stairs tells you *where* the girl ran. It modifies the verb *ran* and answers the question *where*. Thus it takes the part of an adverb.

EXERCISE 118

Make up sentences using the following groups of words. These contain adverb phrases which modify a verb. Write your sentences on the lines below.

1. jumped off the cliff

____

____

2. shook with laughter

____

____

3. waited at the gate

____

____

4. screamed with terror

____

____

5. woven by hand

____

____

In each sentence you have written above, circle the prepositional phrase and draw an arrow to the verb it modifies.

Review of Phrases

A preposition is a little word used with a noun to form a prepositional phrase. The phrase tells *what, when, where,* or *how*. The noun is called the object of the preposition.

EXERCISE 119

In the following sentences, circle each prepositional phrase and draw an arrow to the word it modifies.

Example

Joan played in the garden.

1. The woman waited at the door. __________
2. The lamb followed the farmer to the barn.

   ____
3. Julie wore a sweater of pure wool. ________
4. She ran into her house. _______________
5. Jack rode his motorbike down the hill. _____
6. Grandma's trunk is in the attic. _________
7. She has a heart of gold. ______________
8. Susan went through the door. __________
9. The team played in the gym. ___________
10. The horse gallops across the meadow. _____

After each phrase write *adj* or *adv*, depending on what word the preposition modifies.

EXERCISE 120

In the following sentences, circle each prepositional phrase and draw an arrow to the word it modifies.

1. A boy and a girl sat on the beach. _______
2. The girl's hair was the color of corn silk.

   ____
3. The boy lay on his back. _______________

4. They both basked in the sunshine.________
5. The roof of my house is red.____________
6. My evening dress is of white chiffon. _______
7. My mother made it in the evenings. _______
8. She cut it out after work.______________
9. I stitched the seams on the machine._______
10. I got my wish for a long dress.___________

After each phrase write *adj.* or *adv.*, depending upon what word the prepositional phrase modifies.

Analyzing Sentences

EXERCISE 121

Now you are ready to analyze sentences. This means that you can tell what each word in a sentence does—what its job is in the sentence.

Diagram the sentences below. Draw a single line under the subject and a double line under the verb. Circle all the adjectives modifying the subject. Put an *X* on all adverbs modifying the verb.

Example
(The)(slim)(blonde) girl / walked quickly down the street.

1. The shaggy brown dog walked slowly down the road.
2. The thin stooped man with gray hair leaned heavily on his cane.
3. A huge fat woman with a wide smile waddles cheerfully up the steps.
4. Two little boys of eight years raced noisily up the street.
5. The great golden sun rose majestically in the sky.
6. A graceful boat with white sails skims lightly over the waves.
7. The frightened cat leaped frantically for the door.
8. A crying baby wailed pathetically in the night.
9. Four workers from the farm jump quickly onto the truck.
10. The big friendly coach speaks encouragingly in the locker room.

EXERCISE 122

Now that you have shown which are the nouns and verbs and adjectives and adverbs, go back over the above sentences and see what words are left. You will find, if you have made no mistakes, that you have only prepositional phrases left. Write each phrase on the lines below. At the right write the word each one describes. Then you can tell whether it acts as an adjective or an adverb. Write *adj* or *adv* in the column on the far right.

	PHRASE	WORD IT DESCRIBES	ADJ. OR ADV.
1.	________	________	____
2.	________	________	____
3.	________	________	____
4.	________	________	____
5.	________	________	____
6.	________	________	____
7.	________	________	____
8.	________	________	____
9.	________	________	____
10.	________	________	____
11.	________	________	____
12.	________	________	____
13.	________	________	____
14.	________	________	____
15.	________	________	____

Chapter 13

Still More Punctuation

Apostrophes

An apostrophe, for all its big name, is a little mark like a comma, except that it is placed *above* the word, as in *it's*.

Apostrophes are used *to show possession.* Coming after a singular noun, the apostrophe is followed by an *s*, as in "the girl's hair," to refer to one girl to whom the hair belongs. Since plural nouns usually end in an *s*, the apostrophe after that final *s*, as in "the girls' apartment," indicates that more than one girl owns the apartment.

When the plural form is irregular, and does not end in an *s*, as in the words we have already studied (see Chapter 2), the possessive is formed by adding an apostrophe and an *s*, just as singular possessives are formed.

Example

The man's shoe
The men's shoes

Here, the word *men* already means more than one man and does not need an *s* added to make it plural. The rule holds true for *men*, *women*, and *children,* as well as for *mice* and *geese*.

Another use for apostrophes is to indicate when parts of words are left out or contracted into a shorter form. Words such as *I'll* for *I will* or *can't* for *cannot* are called *contractions*. They are shortened by dropping out letters, and this is indicated by the use of the apostrophe. Contractions help to eliminate many long verb phrases: *Should not have* becomes *shouldn't have*. One frequently misspelled contraction is *doesn't*, short for *does not*. An irregular one is *won't*, short for *will not*. The correct contraction for *I am not* is *I'm not*, although *ain't* is frequently used in common speech.

One common contraction is *it's*, short for *it is*. It is frequently confused with *its*, which is a possessive adjective meaning *belonging to* and which is always followed by the noun it modifies.

Example

It's going to rain. (It is going to rain.)
The train jumped its track. (belonging to the train)

Other possessive adjectives include *my*, *your*, *his*, *her*, *our*, and *their*. None of them has an apostrophe, nor does *its*.

Read the examples below and do the exercises to help you understand apostrophes.

Apostrophes in Possessives

Apostrophes are used

1. to show possession.
2. for contractions.

1. The apostrophe before the *s* shows singular possession (owned by one person).

Example

That boy's work is very good.

2. The apostrophe after the *s* shows plural possession (owned by more than one).

Example

The boys' playthings were all over the floor.

3. Words which have irregular plurals that do not end in *s* are treated like singular nouns.

Example

The women's club had a meeting.

EXERCISE 123

Write the possessive for each of the following nouns and, in the blanks following them, supply something that belongs to the noun, as in the following examples.

Example

George's bicycle
The children's shoes
The dog's collar

1. Mr. Blake ______________________
2. The man ______________________
3. The girl ______________________
4. The girls ______________________
5. The lady ______________________
6. The ladies ______________________
7. The men ______________________
8. Father ______________________
9. The child ______________________
10. The children ______________________

EXERCISE 124

Punctuate the following sentences and watch for the possessives, remembering to notice whether they are singular or plural.

1. Peters book lay on the teachers desk
2. The workers mass meeting lasted a long time
3. Have you seen Joans mother she asked
4. His cars brakes were not working
5. Their cars floodlights blinded him
6. The childrens voices were too loud
7. The unions rules have to be strict
8. This is the club members project to raise money
9. Mr. Blakes house is on the hill
10. Are the womens plans completed

Apostrophes in Contractions

Apostrophes are used

1. for contractions.
2. to show possession.

Study the short or contracted form for each of the following. Note that in the negative forms using *not* the apostrophe usually stands for the *o* in *not* which is dropped. For example, *is not* becomes *isn't*.

Cross out the letters that are dropped in the left hand columns and add apostrophes to make each phrase match the contraction in the right hand column.

Example

I'~~ha~~ve I've

I am	I'm	Where is	Where's
You are	You're	I would	I'd
He is	He's	I will	I'll
She is	She's	I have	I've
It is	It's	You have	You've
We are	We're	We will	We'll
They are	They're	What is	What's

Negative contractions

will not	won't	have not	haven't
does not	doesn't	should not	shouldn't
do not	don't	did not	didn't
can not	can't	would not	wouldn't

EXERCISE 125

Write the contractions for the following:

1. you are ______
2. do not ______
3. it is ______
4. were not ______
5. would not ______
6. can not ______
7. I am ______
8. they are ______
9. we are ______
10. I will ______
11. should not ______
12. will not ______
13. does not ______
14. he is ______
15. I have ______
16. could not ______
17. where is ______
18. I would ______
19. we will ______
20. you have ______

EXERCISE 126

In the blanks, write the contractions which could be used in the sentences.

Example
You should not do that. *shouldn't*

1. He is not ready to go yet.______
2. Do not you have dinner ready yet?______
3. I am as hungry as a bear!______
4. It was not a hard test.______
5. We are not going this week.______
6. I will go with you when you do go.______
7. They would not listen to directions.______
8. He does not understand English very well.
______
9. I can not explain the lesson to him.______
10. It is a beautiful day!______

Remember that:

isn't, hasn't, wasn't } refer to one person.

aren't, haven't, weren't } usually refer to more than one person.

EXERCISE 127

Make up sentences using the following contractions.

1. weren't ______
2. shouldn't ______
3. I'll ______

4. wasn't ______________________

5. you're ______________________

6. don't ______________________

7. we're ______________________

8. hasn't ______________________

9. isn't ______________________

10. doesn't ______________________

EXERCISE 128

Use the following contractions correctly in sentences.

1. can't ______________________

2. haven't ______________________

3. they're ______________________

4. you've ______________________

5. wouldn't ______________________

6. you'll ______________________

7. I've ______________________

8. he's ______________________

9. I'm ______________________

10. she'll ______________________

Still More Troublemakers: Its and It's

Its and *it's* are often confused. The contraction for *it is* is spelled with an apostrophe, *it's*. But the possessive *its*, meaning *belonging to it*, is spelled without an apostrophe and is always followed by a noun. Whenever you use *its*, try substituting *it is* in the sentence. If it makes sense, put in the apostrophe. If it doesn't, leave it out.

Example

It's a lovely day. (It is)
The dog wagged its tail. (<u>not</u> it is)

EXERCISE 129

Change *it is* to *it's* in the following sentences by crossing out the *i* and putting in the apostrophe.

1. It is very cold.
2. It is too late now.
3. It is a beautiful day.
4. Why, it is nearly lunchtime!
5. I like it because it is funny.
6. Drink this. It is delicious!
7. Now it is time to go.
8. It is going to be such fun!
9. It is hard to spell that word.
10. It is not necessary to be rude.

EXERCISE 130

In the following sentences, put an apostrophe in *its* wherever *it is* is meant.

1. Its time to start the meeting.
2. The bus is behind its schedule.
3. Its going to take fifteen minutes.
4. The cat chased its tail.
5. Meat loses its flavor when its cooked too long.
6. Its a nice house; its lawn is lovely, too.
7. The cat carried its kittens in its mouth.

8. The chair has lost one of its legs because its so old.

9. Its going to take an hour for the train to get to its destination.

10. The dog can't find its bone because its under the refrigerator.

Colons and Semicolons

We have learned all about periods, commas, quotation marks, and apostrophes. The only punctuation marks we have not discussed are colons and semicolons.

A *colon* is two periods, one above the other like this: it is used chiefly before a list or a lengthy formal statement.

Example

We have studied the geography of the following countries: Germany, France, Spain, Holland, Belgium, Norway.

A *semicolon* is a half-period; it is a period with a comma under it. It is used to join two short sentences together.

Example

I called loudly; there was no answer.

EXERCISE 131

Put colons or semicolons where needed in the following sentences.

1. He crawled into the cave he looked around.

2. The teacher glanced at the clock it was nearly noon.

3. These boys made the first team Joe Ferrara, Tony Rocci, Henry Koch, Ed Argento.

4. The girl looked at him she said nothing.

5. On her grocery list were written these items apples, milk, lettuce, cereal, steak.

6. The men shouted angrily then the women screamed back at them.

7. The manager ordered the following supplies pencils, pads, carbon paper, tape, stencils.

8. Don't cry, Tommy crying won't help.

9. It was terribly hot the streets were deserted.

10. The instruments in his band were drums, a piano, a bass sax, an electric guitar, and an electric organ.

EXERCISE 132

Put all necessary punctuation in the following sentences.

1. I finished the job however I have not been paid

2. I wish to order the following four lamb chops two packages of peas one quart of milk and one head of lettuce

3. These are the books I have read this year Robinson Crusoe The Legend of Sleepy Hollow David Copperfield The Last of the Mohicans

4. My shoes are old scuffed and dirty his are brand new

5. Why O why cant I ever do anything right

6. Hear us O Lord when we cry unto Thee let our prayers be answered

7. My name is Dr J S Wilson I live at 10 Woodridge Road Chicago Ill

8. These are my favorite foods bananas peanut butter roast beef string beans and cherry pie

9. When the light turns red you stop when it is green you may go

10. The days of the week are abbreviated as follows Sun Mon Tues Wed Thurs Fri Sat

Review Test of Capitals and Punctuation

EXERCISE 133

A. Put capitals and punctuation in all *complete* sentences below.

1. after parking his car, the man
2. the boys went out to play football
3. raced across the tennis court
4. going to the window, Joan
5. opening the door quietly, the mother tiptoed into the room
6. the women gave a shower for Debbie
7. the fun began when
8. when all the presents were opened, the women
9. then they all helped to clean up
10. after the party Kathie and Sue

B. Look at the incomplete sentences. Do you know what is missing? See if you can finish the sentences so that they are complete and make sense.

C. Put capitals and punctuation where needed in the following sentences.

1. christmas day is on thursday december 25
2. oh i didnt know it comes so soon
3. well I still have to shop for my mother my father and my girl friend
4. I hope uncle oscar arrived safely
5. my friend patty has invited me to a holiday party
6. its going to be such fun she said
7. my supervisor mrs newton lives at 83 davis st greenville mass
8. her daughter carol newton is a good friend of mine
9. we were both born on aug 22 1962
10. we did not know each other however until last year

D. Put capitals and punctuation in the following sentences.

1. tony have you loaded that truck asked the boss
2. the winter months are december january and february
3. its so hot outside i had to come in
4. bless me o lord and answer my prayer
5. the letter is dated saturday sept 9 1981
6. my favorite meal is hamburgers baked beans and a glass of milk
7. our cat a siamese has blue eyes

8. its fur is long soft and fluffy

9. i called and called said the boy but nobody answered

10. the boys voice however couldnt be heard over the radios blasting

E. Put apostrophes in the proper places.

1. girls team
2. childrens toys
3. cant talk
4. mens coats
5. ladies dresses
6. babys bottle
7. doesnt drive
8. sheeps wool
9. havent got
10. youll go

Give yourself 3 points for each sentence above and 1 point for each item in part E. Take off 1 point for each error. Be sure to review anything that gives you trouble before you go on.

Chapter 14

Conjunctions and Interjections

The last two parts of speech that we have to learn are *conjunctions* and *interjections.*

The hardest things about these little words are their names. That's because they're based on Latin; so naturally they are harder for us than English. Now let's learn a little Latin!

Con means *with,* and *junction* means *joined—joined with.* A junction is a station where different railroad lines connect. Just as two railroad lines connect at the junction, so two sentences are connected by conjunctions. *And* is the most commonly used conjunction. Subjects connected by *and* are called *compound subjects* (see Chapter 1). In the same way, sentences connected by *and* are called *compound sentences.*

Example

(Compound subject) (Compound sentence)
Mary *and* Jane shopped *and* then they went home.

An injection is a shot. What do we say when we get a shot? *Ouch! Ow! Eek! Wow!* and maybe *Whew!* when it is over. These words are all *interjections. Inter* means *into* or *between* and *jection* means *shot.* They are shot into the sentence to express strong feeling. Usually they stand alone, though sometimes they are actually between *(inter)* the words of the sentence.

Example

Nuts! I forgot my lunch!
I fear, alas, that all is lost.
Hear us, O Lord, when we cry to Thee.

Conjunctions

Conjunctions are bridge words. They join words and sentences together the way a bridge connects islands. The conjunctions most frequently used are

and but
or because
so for

A conjunction may connect

1) nouns in a compound subject.

Example

Susan *and* Gladys are there.

2) verbs in a compound predicate.

Example

The cheerleaders yelled *and* shouted.

3) Two separate sentences in a compound sentence.

Example

Tom / rang the bell, *and* my brother / opened the door.

EXERCISE 134

Separate these compound sentences into two parts and draw a line between them. Circle all the conjunctions. You should be able to find ten of them.

Example
He went home / (and) called up his friend.

1. My parents love me but they get angry at me.
2. Do your work well or you will be fired.
3. He missed his train, for his taxi was caught in heavy traffic.
4. Jim wanted a new bike but he couldn't afford one.
5. The next Friday was his birthday so his father bought one for him.
6. We went to the clambake and Charlie ate at least ninety clams.
7. I like the meat but I don't want the vegetables.
8. You must practice hard or you won't do well.
9. We waited a long time, for Hal was late.
10. Then the door opened and he walked in.

EXERCISE 135

In each line below are two short sentences. Rewrite them, using the conjunction that follows the end of the sentence to make one smooth sentence instead of two short, choppy ones.

Example
The baby cried. His mother came. *so*
The baby cried so his mother came.

1. I am late. I lost my way. *because*
2. You go now. I'll come later. *and*
3. The game was over. I went home. *so*
4. The bell rang. No one answered it. *but*
5. Mary ran to the door. She knew who was there! *for*
6. Mrs. Smith took the inventory. Then she ordered more supplies. *and*
7. Debbie baked a pie. They would have dessert. *so*
8. Get out of here. Don't come back. *and*
9. It didn't hurt at first. Later it hurt a lot. *but*
10. I couldn't do my homework. I didn't have time. *because*

Interjections

EXERCISE 136

Interjections are the Lone Rangers of our language. They stand alone, usually separated by an exclamation mark. They modify nothing and have no job in the sentence except to express strong feeling or excitement as in *Oh!*, *Ouch!*, and *Wow! Oh* is sometimes spelled without the *h* when used with a noun of address.

Example

Hear us, O Lord, when we cry unto Thee.
Wow! Look at that!

Underline the interjections in the sentences below.

1. "Bah and humbug!" said Scrooge.
2. Lo, a miracle happened!
3. Oh, my! I almost forgot!
4. Nuts! I should have known better.
5. Whew! That was a narrow escape!
6. Alas, we must say farewell.
7. Hurray! We won the lottery!
8. Hey, wait for me!
9. Have mercy upon us, O Lord!
10. Ouch! I cut my finger!

EXERCISE 137

Put capitals and punctuation in the following sentences.

1. my goodness i forgot my dental appointment
2. hey where do you think youre going
3. good lord whats going on here
4. hear my prayer o lord and be merciful
5. pow robert hit the crook hard
6. ding dong the bells are ringing
7. gee whiz thats not fair
8. the boy fired his toy gun bang and the bird flew away
9. boy you made a strike
10. we won hurray for our team

Review of Prepositions, Conjunctions, and Interjections

EXERCISE 138

What part of speech is followed by a noun, forming a phrase?____________________

What part of speech expresses excitement or emotion?____________________

What part of speech joins words and groups of words in a sentence?________________

Diagram the following sentences; notice that some are compound sentences. Circle each prepositional phrase and draw an arrow to the word it modifies.

1. The police in the patrol car drove down the road.
2. Ouch! I caught my finger in the door!
3. Pete and Dave fished in the river.
4. The girls on the stage sang and danced before the audience.
5. The food was very hot, but it was tasty.
6. The foreman was very strict in the factory.

7. On the street, though, he laughed and fooled with the workers.

8. I took my brother to the circus on his birthday.

9. Gee, we ate lots of popcorn, for it was delicious!

10. I liked all the animals, but the elephants were the best in the show.

From the sentences above, select two examples of each of the following and write them in the spaces provided.

1. Prepositional phrases used as adjectives.

____

____

2. Prepositional phrases used as adverbs.

____

____

3. Interjections.__________ __________

4. Conjunctions used with compound subjects and predicates.__________ __________

5. Conjunctions used to join two complete sentences.__________ __________

Review

We have now learned all the eight parts of speech used in our language. Let us review them.

Noun—refers to a person, place, or thing, including things you cannot touch such as *love* or *anger*. Times and seasons such as *noon, Tuesday,* or *autumn* are also nouns.
Pronoun—stands in place of a noun and refers back to it.
Verb—expresses action or being
Adjective—describes a noun or a pronoun.
Adverb—describes a verb, an adjective, or another adverb.
Preposition—forms a phrase with the noun which is its object.
Conjunction—joins words or sentences together.
Interjection—expresses excitement or emotion.

Sometimes the same word may be used in different ways. You have to decide what function a word has in a sentence before you can name what part of speech it is.

Examples

Her mother packed her summer clothes.

(*Summer* is an adjective describing the noun *clothes.)*

Summer is my favorite season of the year.
(In this sentence, *summer* is a noun, the subject of the sentence.)

His *work* is very difficult.
(Here, *work* is a noun, the subject of the sentence.)
They *work* all day in the fields.
(In this case, *work* is a verb expressing action.)

Parts of Speech

EXERCISE 139

Read the following sentences carefully. It may help to diagram them. The underlined words serve different functions in different sentences. After each sentence write what part of speech the underlined word is in that particular sentence.

1. I love my children. __________
2. Love is a wonderful feeling.__________
3. The children taste the new dessert.__________
4. My sister has good taste in clothes.__________
5. My mattress has a broken spring.__________
6. All the flowers bloom in the spring.__________

7. The kids spring on the trampoline.________

8. We went to a dance last night.____________

9. They dance well together.________________

10. I would enjoy his talk if he didn't talk so much.______________________________

9. Roger put the money in his pants pocket.
____

10. The dog pants for water because he is hot.
____

EXERCISE 140

After each sentence write what part of speech the underlined word is in that particular sentence.

1. I played with him during the noon recess.
____

2. My mother came home at noon.________

3. The dog barks at the child.____________

4. His bark is worse than his bite. _________

5. The ring of the bell woke Jerry.__________

6. Please ring for the nurse.______________

7. My shirt is made of cotton.____________

8. Janet wore a new cotton dress.__________

A Reminding Rhyme

You have learned what each word in a sentence is and what its job is in making a complete sentence. The rhyme below will help you remember what you have learned.

A *noun's* a person, place, or thing,
Or sometimes even time, like spring.
A *verb* tells what the subject does,
Like "jumps" or "fishes," "is" or "was."
An *adjective* describes a noun,
Like "gay" or "ugly," "rich" or "brown."
An *adverb* tells you how or when,
Like "quietly" or "well" or "then."
A *pronoun* takes the noun's own place,
Like "they" for "children," "she" for "Grace."
A *preposition* leads a noun:
"In bed," "at sea," or "to the town."
Conjunctions are a bridge across
Two sentences: "but," "and," "because."
The *interjections,* last of all,
Like "Oh!" and "Ouch!" are very small.

Chapter 15

Letter Writing

Letters are very important in our society. We write friendly letters to our friends and family and business letters to companies about various matters. A well-written letter should express the writer's thoughts clearly. This chapter contains good examples of both friendly and business letters.

There are differences in style between friendly and business letters. Study the models below before you compose your own. You have already learned the use of capitals and commas in punctuation; note, however, that no periods are used in the heading of a letter.

Friendly Letter

Heading⟶ 3 Rutland Road
Great Neck, N. Y. 11405
Dec. 11, 19——

Greeting⟶ Dear Dave,

Body:

It has been a long time since I've seen you. In all this ice and snow, last summer seems very far away. But I haven't forgotten what a good time we had.

My Christmas vacation begins next week, on December 18. Why don't you come and visit me? Bring your skates because the ice is perfect now. If it snows again, we can go to New Hampshire for a day or two of skiing.

Please write soon, and tell me that you'll come. We could have a great time.

Closing⟶ Always your friend,
Signature⟶ Joe

Heading: This is the writer's address and the date on which the letter was written. Often the writer's address is printed on his stationery, in which case only the date needs to be written in the upper right-hand corner.

Greeting: This depends on the relationship between the writers. The writer might begin "My dear Aunt Sally" or "Dear Miss Neary." The first word is capitalized, as is the name of the person written to. The greeting may be followed by either a comma or a colon, but in friendly letters commas are used more often.

Body: A handwritten letter should be indented at the beginning of each paragraph. A margin of about an inch should be left on the left-hand side to make the letter look neat and evenly spaced.

Closing: This is indented about halfway across the page and is followed by a comma. Its wording also depends on the writer's mood and relationship to his correspondent. The closing might read, "With love," "Affectionately," "Lovingly," "Always yours," or just "Yours." To someone who is not a close friend or relative, the closing would read "Yours truly," "Yours sincerely," or "Very truly yours," just as in a formal business letter.

Signature: This should be centered beneath the closing and may consist of just the writer's first name or his full name, depending on how well he knows the person to whom he is writing. You would not, of course, sign your full name when writing to your parents or to your girl friend. The signature should always be handwritten, whether the letter is written or typed.

An envelope should be addressed in the lower right-hand quarter, if the spacing permits. The longer the address, of course, the further toward the left it will have to begin. The writer's address should be in the upper left-hand corner. The stamp should be neatly placed in the upper right-hand corner.

J. Wiley, Jr.
3 Rutland Rd.
Great Neck, N.Y. 11405

Mr. David Williams
42 Locust Ave.
Gloversville
New York 12735

Envelopes for business letters are addressed in the same way. The title of the person to whom you are writing is given, if you know it, followed by the name of the firm. The writer's return address should always be in the upper left-hand corner.

J. Wiley, Jr.
3 Rutland Rd.
Great Neck, N.Y. 11405

stamp

Mr. John M. Williams, President
Creative Concerns, Inc.
549 Fifth Ave.
New York, N.Y. 10016

Business Letter

Business letters are usually typed in single space, with inch-wide margins. Between paragraphs, leave two spaces. The paragraphs and closing are indented the same as in a friendly letter. Recently, however, many business firms have been using a newer form without indentations. A sample of this modern style is shown in the letter below. In either case, the letter is signed by hand above the typewritten signature, so be sure to leave four spaces after the closing before typing the signature.

The following is a sample business letter:

3290 49th Avenue
Rome, Ohio 10035
July 29, 19——

Acme Electronic Company
1479 Davis Street
St. Louis, Texas 10029

Dear Sir:

On June 10 I ordered pocket calculator #SB-47763-4 from your catalog, but an error was made in the shipment I received. The pocket calculator that was sent to me was #SB-47765-2, which I am returning to you. Please send me the pocket calculator that I originally ordered. Thank you for your cooperation.

Yours truly,

Carl Gutterman

Carl Gutterman

Heading: In a business letter from a private person, the heading is typed on the right as in a friendly letter.

Greeting: The greeting is preceded by the formal name and address of the firm to whom the letter is written. If the letter is written to a specific person, his name is given first. The greeting is formal: "Gentlemen:" or "Dear Sir:" or "Dear Madam:" is appropriate.

Body: The body of the letter is brief and to the point. If you are writing to order merchandise, always state clearly the model, number, and price of the items ordered. Allow enough for postage and taxes, and specify how you want the goods shipped. If you are writing to complain about poor merchandise received, be sure to give all the above information and your order number.

Closing: This is formal and does not vary much. "Yours truly," "Yours sincerely," or "Very truly yours" are standard closings.

Signature: The signature is handwritten above the typed signature; leave four spaces between the closing and the typed signature.

Job Application Letter

There are several important things to remember when writing a job application letter. First, your letter should be brief and should follow the format of a regular business letter. If you are answering an advertisement that appeared in a newspaper or magazine, be sure to state exactly where and when you saw the ad. Next, give your prospective employer some information about yourself, for example, your educational background and your previous work experience. Also, list any skills you have that would be useful for the particular job you're interested in. Finally, tell your prospective employer how he or she can get in touch with you for an interview. The following is an example of a job application letter:

1042 Dayton Avenue
Kansas City, Kansas 67911
December 3, 19——

Director of Personnel
Randall Advertising Agency, Inc.
1405 Harcross Boulevard
Kansas City, Kansas 67932

Dear Sir:

I am writing in response to your advertisement for a receptionist which appeared in the November 29th issue of the *Kansas City Star*.

I am a recent high school graduate and am very interested in the advertising field. Because I enjoy working with people, I feel that I could perform the duties of a receptionist well. I would like the opportunity to put into practice the business procedures and typing skills I learned while in school.

I am available for an interview at your convenience. You may reach me between 9:00 A.M. and 5:00 P.M. at 967-2931. I look forward to hearing from you.

Sincerely,

Jane Gray

Jane Gray

Notice that the style of this letter is direct and to the point. The writer tells what skills and qualities she has to offer her prospective employer. She also states how she can be reached during the day. If you have any previous work experience, be sure to describe it briefly and give references with telephone numbers where possible. Good luck!

Chapter 16

Final Review

EXERCISE 141

A. Do you remember the four kinds of sentences? After each sentence write the initial for the kind of sentence it is. If in doubt review Chapter 5.

1. What a beautiful day! ________________
2. It's too nice to stay inside. ______________
3. Go on out and get some exercise. _______
4. Don't you want to go out? _____________
5. I'll help you with your homework later. _____
6. What are you waiting for? ______________
7. Help me carry these packages. _________ ______________________________________
8. What's the matter? Don't you feel well? ____ ______________________________________
9. Quick, call a doctor! _________________
10. I knew something was wrong. ___________

B. Put capitals and punctuation where needed in the following sentences.

1. peter david and jeff are brothers
2. they live at 35 spring st houston tex
3. peter the oldest was born on Apr 21 1965
4. jimmy will you please come here called his friend
5. i cant now joe shouted jimmy im right in the middle of this
6. its all right said his friend i found what i wanted
7. the minister rev carey came into the room
8. she put the camera back in its case
9. mens shoes and ladies hats are on the fifth floor
10. o lord what am i going to do now she sighed

C. In the following sentences, write the correct word in the blank space.

1. We went to ___________ house for dinner. (their, there)
2. Betsy has done her work _________. (good, well)
3. It's __________ cold __________ go outside. (too, to, two)

4. __________ are some good books here but this one is the __________. (their, there; better, best)

5. Doris grows more __________ every day. (lovely, lovelier)

More Final Review

EXERCISE 142

Diagram the following sentences. Remember the subject of an imperative sentence is implied (you).

1. Oh, the needles and pins are in my workbox.
2. Mr. Baldwin, the president, came into the office.
3. The clerks listened very quietly to him.
4. He lectured and scolded them.
5. A flock of geese flew over the trees.
6. The dark leaden sky was heavy with rain.
7. Joe, please pass the bread.
8. Jerry is the strongest boy on the team.
9. High in the sky the sun shone.
10. There is Mrs. Kaufman, our neighbor.

From the sentences above, choose and give examples of the following:

1. A singular common noun __________
2. A plural common noun __________
3. A proper noun __________
4. A compound subject __________
5. A compound verb __________
6. A predicate noun __________
7. A noun of address __________
8. An appositive noun __________
9. A collective noun __________
10. A verb of being, present tense __________
11. A verb of action, past tense __________
12. A direct object __________
13. A predicate adjective __________
14. A pronoun as subject __________
15. A pronoun as object __________
16. A prepositional phrase modifying a noun __________
17. An adverb modifying a verb __________
18. An adverb modifying another adverb __________
19. An interjection __________
20. A conjunction __________
21. A prepositional phrase modifying a verb __________
22. Give the present tense of *flew* __________
23. Give the present tense of *shone* __________
24. Give the "most" form of an adjective __________
25. Give an irregular plural noun __________

Final Test

EXERCISE 143

A. Put capitals and punctuation in the following sentences.

1. pete are you going to the baseball game asked ted
2. who wants to watch the mets lose again said pete
3. oh well said ted its better than staying home watching television
4. tomorrow is my birthday i was born on tues aug 31 1955
5. when i was small we lived in chicago at 151 spring st
6. my uncles car hasnt a spare tire
7. dr spencer came to dinner on thanksgiving day
8. my boss mr j f morris doesnt take any nonsense
9. bobbys little brothers are jimmy arthur and dick
10. the boys bats and mitts lay all over the porch

B. Correct any incomplete or run-on sentences. Add words or punctuation if necessary. After each sentence write the initial for the kind of sentence it is.

1. I washed the dishes and made the beds then I vacuumed the rug.______________
2. What a lot of work you did!___________
3. Did your mother thank you?__________
4. Stop making so much noise.__________
5. When I was ready for school ___________

C. Diagram each of the following sentences.

1. The Pope gave his blessing to the crowd.
2. The dog in the last kennel barks loudly.
3. The family spent Labor Day at their grandmother's house.
4. Up the quiet street skipped Julie and Judy, the twins.
5. They laughed and chattered merrily.
6. Their mother called them but they skipped on.
7. We are the two fastest runners on the track team.
8. The boy in the corner is very tall.
9. Millie wants us to go with her.
10. But we are much too busy.

D. From the sentences above, select and write on the space below an example of

1. A proper noun____________________
2. A common singular noun____________
3. A collective noun___________________
4. A noun used as a direct object_________
5. A plural pronoun used as a subject_____
6. A pronoun used as an object___________
7. An adverb modifying a verb__________
8. An adjective modifying a noun_______

9. A predicate nominative______________

10. A compound sentence (give its number)

____

11. A compound subject______________

12. A compound verb______________

13. A verb of being in the present tense____

14. A verb of action in the present tense____

15. A prepositional phrase used as an adjective______________________

16. A prepositional phrase used as an adverb

____

17. A predicate adjective______________

18. A noun in apposition______________

19. An adverb modifying an adjective______

20. A conjunction______________________

E. Give the plurals of

1. policeman______________________
2. family______________________
3. leaf______________________
4. noise______________________
5. mouse______________________

F. Give the present tense of

1. gave______________________
2. spent______________________
3. was______________________
4. sang______________________
5. chattered______________________

G. Compare the following adjectives.

Adjective	*More*	*Most*
1. proud		
2. good		
3. beautiful		
4. merry		
5. bad		

H. Write a different pronoun as a subject for each of the following verbs.

1. ______________ am
2. ______________ are
3. ______________ is
4. ______________ was
5. ______________ were

Scoring: Give 3 points for each sentence in A.
Give 2 points for each sentence in B and C.
Give 1 point for each item in D, E, F, G, and H.
Take off 1 point for each mistake.

If you have over 80 points on this test, you have a good basic understanding of correct English. It will help you to speak and write more effectively. Be sure to correct your mistakes, going back to read the instructions if there is anything you still don't understand.

Conclusions

We have come to the end of a long road. We began with the simplest of two-word sentences, gradually building up an understanding of long compound sentences with perhaps two or three subjects or verbs. We have studied all eight parts of speech so that you understand what function each one performs in the construction of a sentence.

As we explained in the Introduction, English is a very complicated language which has come down to us from ancient sources. There are many more irregularities and complicated forms than we have been able to cover in this book. In some cases we have overlooked exceptions to the rules, and we have simplified more difficult subjects, such as compound verb forms. But with this basic knowledge as an introduction, you can go on and increase your knowledge further if you wish to.

This has been hard work, but you will find it has been worth the effort. If you have done the work well, you should now have a much better understanding of how to construct good simple English sentences. You can have confidence in your ability to communicate clearly and correctly. This will help you in your day-to-day work and give you more enjoyment in your communications with others. May the efforts you put into this work bring you success and satisfaction.

M. A. P.

Answer Key for Exercises

EXERCISE 1

S P
1. Fish/swim.
2. Bees/buzz.
3. Birds/fly.
4. Babies/cry.
5. Cats/purr.
6. Trains/run.
7. Planes/fly.
8. Boats/sail.
9. Wood/burns.
10. Children/play.

EXERCISE 2

1. The snow/fell.
2. A flower/bloomed.
3. The girl/cried.
4. The food/smelled good.
5. A boy/yelled.
6. The car/speeds by.
7. The man/whistled softly.
8. A girl/laughed.
9. The bells/rang loudly.
10. The clock/struck ten.

EXERCISE 3

1. The boys played baseball.
2. A dog barked far away.
3. The car speeded past.
4. A policeman stopped it.
5. The driver looked unhappy.
6. The ticket cost him ten dollars.
7. An apple rolled off the table.
8. The women shopped for bargains.
9. Jimmy loves to fish.
10. An eagle soared across the sky.

EXERCISE 4

1. The clouds gathered in the east.
2. A plane roared overhead.

3. The flowers wilted without water.

4. The telephone rang for a long time.

5. An ostrich has long legs.

6. The traffic grew much heavier.

7. Alice danced around the room.

8. An umbrella keeps off the rain.

9. The students did their homework.

10. A lady wrote to her son.

Check your answer key carefully. Did you find all the subjects correctly? How many subjects were preceded by *a*? 2 How many by *an*? 2 Write the vowels at the beginnings of the words preceded by *an*. o, u

EXERCISE 5
(Suggested Subjects)

1. The girl /walked into the pizza parlor.
2. The man /handed out hundred dollar bills.
3. The dog /growled furiously outside the door.
4. A cat /chased the frightened child.
5. The child /sits under a tree and dreams.
6. The thief /drove a big blue Cadillac.
7. The shovel /dug deep into the soft earth.
8. The clown /wore a crazy flowered hat.
9. An actor /stalked across the empty stage.
10. The man /shouted angrily at the boy.

The	A	An
8	1	1

EXERCISE 6

1. The boy / dialed the wrong number.

2. The painter / fell off the ladder.

3. The chef / prepares a delicious meal.

4. The family / ate dinner at the new restaurant.

5. A dog / chases a squirrel in the park.

6. An artist / drew a sketch of the old bridge.

7. The elephant / escapes from the zoo.

8. An apple / falls from the tree.

9. The dentist / filled the cavity quickly.

10. The elevator / stopped on the tenth floor.

EXERCISE 7
(Suggested Predicates)

1. The hairy monster / attacked the village.
2. An astronaut / walked on the moon.
3. The fat old lady / ate the pizza.
4. A green sports car / turned the corner.
5. The husky policeman / wrote a ticket.
6. My grandmother / bakes cookies.
7. The tall waiter / served dinner.
8. The girl's blonde hair / looked fake.
9. The frightened horse / reared.
10. The baseball team / won the game.

EXERCISE 8

Every sentence must have:

1. A subject which performs the action. It is called a noun.
2. A predicate which describes the action the subject does. The main word is a verb.

1. Frank/whistled.
2. The birds/sang.
3. The employees/ate lunch.
4. Our team/won.
5. Mary/fed her cat.
6. Joe/dropped his hammer.
7. The clock/stopped.
8. A bell/rang.
9. The sun/shone in the sky.
10. Flowers/blossom in spring.
11. The moon/rose across the lake.
12. The canoe/glided down the river.
13. The red car/roared down the street.
14. Ed/hit the ball hard.
15. The boys/played a game.
16. The passengers/lined up quickly.
17. The supervisor/handed out the paychecks.
18. The big black dog/chased me away.
19. The goldfish/swims around the pond.
20. The shining stars/gleam in the sky.

EXERCISE 9

1. Fish/swim all over the lake.
2. Bees/buzz around the flowers all day.
3. Birds/fly south in the winter.
4. Babies/cry when they are hungry.
5. Cats/purr deep down in their throats.
6. Trains/run from Boston to California.
7. Planes/fly very low over the airport.
8. Boats/sail up and down the lake.
9. Plants/need sunlight and water.
10. Children/play in the park.

EXERCISE 10

1. The snow/fell three feet deep last night.
2. A red flower/bloomed in her garden.
3. The girl/cried because she couldn't go.
4. The food/smelled good to the hungry men.
5. A boy/yelled at the big bully.
6. The foreign car/speeds by with the police after it.
7. The man/whistled softly to himself.
8. A girl/laughed at his joke.
9. The church bells/rang loudly on Sunday morning.
10. The clock/struck ten in the empty old house.

EXERCISE 11

1. The big gray cat/sat on the fence.
2. Thick white snowflakes/drifted down.
3. A very tall boy/ran across the street.

S P
4. A big red car/roared down the highway.

S P
5. A police car/speeded after it.

S P
6. A fat old lady/rocked the baby.

S P
7. The shouting boys/skated in the park.

S P
8. A sleepy old man/opened the door.

S P
9. Two tired children/crawled into bed.

S P
10. The red-headed girl/spells very well.

EXERCISE 12

2. telephone	7. street
3. team	8. dog
5. house	10. hero
7. car	10. day

S P
1. The young actor/combed his hair.

S P
2. My sister/answered the telephone.

S P
3. Our football team/beat the other team.

S P
4. Our coach/praised our good playing.

S P
5. The silent thief/sneaked into the house.

S P
6. The big watchdog/barked at him.

S P
7. A policeman/drove his car up the street.

S P
8. The sneaky thief/ran away from the dog.

S P
9. The policeman/grabbed him as he ran.

S P
10. The watchdog/became the hero of the day.

EXERCISE 13

CS
1. Rachel and Bill/took a taxi home.

CP
2. The audience/cheers and claps for the actor.

CS
3. Mike, Tom, and Betsy/organized the meeting.

CP
4. The young man/slips and falls on the ice.

CS
5. The car and the bike/collided at the light.

CP
6. The guests/laugh and dance at the party.

CS
7. Nancy and her sister/left early.

CP
8. They/bought groceries and cooked dinner.

CP
9. Mary/opened the door and walked into the room.

CS
10. Steve and his girl friend/had an argument.

EXERCISE 14
(Suggested Answers)

1. Beth and Jane went shopping.
2. Ships and airplanes hasten travel.
3. Dogs and cats often fight.
4. Thunder and lightning frightened her.
5. Men and women enjoy tennis.

Write sentences using the following *compound predicates:*

1. The girl danced and sang.
2. The boys run and jump.
3. The wrestler struggled and sweated.
4. The children told jokes and played games.
5. Jim jumped into the water and swam.

EXERCISE 15

S P

1. The frightened kitten/crawled under the bed.

S P

2. The cross old lady/scolded the waiter.

S P

3. Torn yellow curtains/hung in the window.

S P

4. The winter wind/shrieked and howled down the alley.

CS P

5. Robins and bluejays/sat in a tree.

S P

6. The excited brown puppy/ran around barking.

S P

7. A beautiful girl/bought the white satin dress.

CS P

8. The fat little boy and his brother/ate the whole cake.

S P

9. A train/whistled loudly.

S P

10. The train/roared into the station.

S P

11. The shining moon/rose over the city.

S P

12. A cherry tree/bloomed in the park.

S P

13. The winter rain/poured down on the earth.

S P

14. The thin man/hurried down the street.

S CP

15. The angry dogs/growled and barked at the stranger.

S P

16. The hungry fish/swim toward the bait.

S P

17. The warm spring sun/shone brightly.

S P

18. The red sports car/roared up the hill.

S P

19. The very exciting game/ended finally.

S CP

20. The noisy boys/shouted and cheered.

EXERCISE 16

S P O

1. The cat/chased a mouse.

S P O

2. His mother/called Tom.

S P O

3. My sister/wore my dress.

S P O

4. The policeman/grabbed the thief.

S P O

5. The firemen/stopped the fire.

S P O

6. His car/hit a tree.

S P O

7. The teacher/graded the papers.

S P O

8. The mother/rocked the baby.

S P O

9. The man/paid his bill.

S P O

10. The wind/rattles the windows.

EXERCISE 17

S P O

1. The dog/gnawed his bone.

S P O

2. A bird/sang a song.

S P O

3. The farmer/planted seed.

S P O

4. Snow/covered the ground.

S P O

5. The ship/hit a reef.

S P O

6. The waves/pounded the rocks.

S P O

7. A jet plane/broke the sound barrier.

S P O

8. The capsule/hit the ocean.

S P O

9. The rocket/missed its target.

S P O

10. A bomb/shattered the building.

EXERCISE 18

X X

1. (Julie) asked her mother for a quarter.

X X

2. The fish swam around the pond.

3. Jonah was swallowed by a whale.
4. The little yellow bird sang in the tree.
5. June is my favorite month.
6. Robert moved to California.
7. His father bought a house in Los Angeles.
8. The picture fell off the wall.
9. Mary asked Grandmother to read her a story.
10. The dog bit the mailman.

EXERCISE 19

1. Patty has a brother named David.
2. A little white rabbit ran across the yard.
3. Central Park is in New York.
4. Mary answered the telephone.
5. The children were going to school.
6. Don plays for the Mets.
7. Abe hit the ball with a stick.
8. The cheerful cook baked a big chocolate cake for Christmas Day.
9. My favorite sports are football, tennis, and track.
10. George, Joe, and Tony have parts in a show on Broadway.

EXERCISE 20

1. The girl bought a hat in the store.
2. The families of the Canadians waited at the airport.
3. The boys played ball with Billy.
4. My home is in Chicago, but I have a bungalow on Lake Erie.
5. Betty dropped a dish on the floor of the restaurant.
6. My cat chased Fido across the grass and down Elm Street.
7. On Sunday the fellows went to Shea Stadium.
8. The wolves howl on the mountains on cold winter nights.
9. John and his brother assembled the Volkswagen.
10. Those boys belong to Little League.

EXERCISE 21

1. George Washington was our first president.
2. Mark Twain and Washington Irving are famous American writers.
3. The Amazon is the longest river in South America.
4. The Giants won the game with the Jets last Saturday.
5. Sons often grow up to be like their fathers.
6. There are many pink flowers on the cherry tree.
7. One tulip bloomed in my garden.

8. (Jupiter)[S] is a planet[XS] with several moons[XP].

9. (Venus)[S] and (Mars)[S] are also planets[XP].

10. We had beef[XS] and potatoes[XP] for dinner[XS].

EXERCISE 22

1. toy ___toys___
2. body ___bodies___
3. guy ___guys___
4. lady ___ladies___
5. fly ___flies___
6. party ___parties___
7. sky ___skies___
8. key ___keys___
9. hobby ___hobbies___
10. story ___stories___

EXERCISE 23

1. chimney ___chimneys___
2. company ___companies___
3. valley ___valleys___
4. pony ___ponies___
5. ray ___rays___
6. bunny ___bunnies___
7. family ___families___
8. delay ___delays___
9. monkey ___monkeys___
10. candy ___candies___

EXERCISE 24

1. trio ___trios___
2. tomato ___tomatoes___
3. rodeo ___rodeos___
4. piano ___pianos___
5. photo ___photos___
6. igloo ___igloos___
7. embargo ___embargoes___
8. auto ___autos___
9. cargo ___cargoes___
10. hero ___heroes___

EXERCISE 25

1. A ___herd___ of cows grazed in the meadow.
2. A ___flock___ of chickens was in the yard.
3. A ___group, class___ of children played in the park.
4. The United States ___Army___ trains its officers at West Point.
5. The ___audience___ in the theater enjoyed the show.
6. The ___congregation___ of the church attended Sunday services.
7. A ___gang, bunch, group___ of boys gathered on the street.
8. A ___grove___ of pine trees grew in the valley.
9. Our baseball ___team___ won the game.
10. My Boy Scout ___troop___ went on a hike.

EXERCISE 26

1. thieves ___thief___

2. women woman
3. houses house
4. mice mouse
5. armies army
6. nations nation
7. pianos piano
8. boxes box
9. children child
10. nurses nurse
11. leaves leaf
12. tomatoes tomato
13. teeth tooth
14. cabbages cabbage
15. horses horse
16. hobbies hobby
17. lice louse
18. knives knife
19. knees knee
20. laces lace

EXERCISE 27

A noun is the name of a person, place, or thing.

1. Sally (S) | wears (P) (slacks) to work.
2. The bird (S) | carried (P) a (worm) to its nest.
3. Frank and Mario (CS) | raced (P) their (cars) down the highway.
4. A policeman (S) | drove (P) his (motorcycle) after them.
5. The tall trooper (S) | gave (P) a (ticket) to each of them.
6. A flock (S) of ducks | waddled (P) across the road.
7. Sandy and Liz (CS) | enjoyed (P) the (movie.)
8. The children (S) | jumped (P) and ran (CP) in the playground.
9. The sun (S) | rose (P) from behind the mountains.
10. The American army (S) | won (P) the (battle.)

Any five of the following are correct.

PROPER NOUNS

Sally	Sandy
Frank	Liz
Mario	

COMMON NOUNS

1. slacks	6. flock, ducks, road
2. bird, worm, nest	7. movie
3. cars, highway	8. children, playground
4. policeman, motorcycle	9. sun, mountains
5. trooper, ticket	10. army, battle

SINGULAR NOUNS	PLURAL NOUNS
all proper nouns plus	slacks, cars,
bird, worm, nest,	ducks, children
highway, policeman,	mountains
motorcycle, trooper	

ticket, flock, road, movie, playground, sun, army, battle

1. A compound subject includes more than one noun.

2. A compound predicate includes more than one verb.

3. A collective noun is singular in form but it includes a number of people or things.

Diagram the following sentences as usual. Put a circle around any objects.

1. A robin (S) | built (P) its (nest) in the tree.
2. The Bermans and the Shaws (CS) | live (P) in Chicago.
3. Julie and Pam (CS) | led (P) the (parade.)
4. The crowd (S) | shouted and screamed (CP).
5. Our team (S) | won (P) three football (games.)
6. A gang (S) of boys | broke (P) (windows) in the school.
7. A policeman (S) | caught and arrested (CP) the (fellows.)
8. Our club (S) | elected (P) a (president) named Joe Ferrara.
9. The astronauts (S) | walked (P) in outer space.
10. The rocket (S) | reached (P) the (moon) safely.

COMPOUND SUBJECT

Bermans and Shaws

Julie and Pam

COMPOUND PREDICATE

shouted and screamed

caught and arrested

COLLECTIVE NOUNS

gang, team,

club, crowd

PROPER	COMMON	SINGULAR	PLURAL
Bermans	robin	robin	Bermans
Shaws	nest	nest	Shaws
Chicago	tree	tree	games
Julie	parade	Chicago	windows
Pam	crowd	Julie	fellows
Joe Ferrara	team	Pam	astronauts
	games	parade	
	gang	crowd	
	boys	team	
	windows	gang	
	school	school	
	policeman	policeman	
	fellows	club	
	club	president	
	president	Joe Ferrara	
	astronauts	space	
	space	rocket	
	rocket	moon	
	moon		

EXERCISE 28

1. Bill chased ___me___ into the house. (I, me)
2. ___I___ began to scream for my mother. (I, Me)
3. ___She___ came running when she heard. (She, Her)
4. Joe and Harry came home for dinner with ___me___. (I, me)
5. My mother cooked a turkey for ___them___. (they, them)
6. After dinner ___we___ all watched TV. (we, us)
7. Do you want to come with ___us___? (we, us)
8. ___We___ are going to a show. (We, Us)
9. ___She___ was wearing a new dress. (She, Her)
10. It looked beautiful on ___her___. (she, her)

EXERCISE 29

1. Polly and ___I___ went swimming. (I, me)
2. ___He___ and Mary went to the movies. (He, Him)
3. They went with my boy friend and ___me___. (I, me)
4. Either Dan or ___I___ will pick you up. (I, me)
5. You can go with ___us___ if you want. (we, us)
6. ___He___ and ___I___ are buddies. (He, Him; I, me)
7. That's secret between you and ___me___. (I, me)
8. They have an agreement among ___them___. (they, them)
9. Both ___she___ and ___I___ were late to school. (she, her; I, me)
10. Was there a quarrel between ___her___ (she, her) and ___him___? (he, him)

EXERCISE 30

	PRESENT TENSE	PAST TENSE
1.	skate	skated
2.	study	studied
3.	buzz	buzzed
4.	bloom	bloomed
5.	whistle	whistled
6.	light	lighted
7.	laugh	laughed
8.	cry	cried
9.	marry	married
10.	wash	washed

EXERCISE 31

	PRESENT TENSE	PAST TENSE
1.	wish	wished
2.	ask	asked
3.	like	liked
4.	try	tried
5.	drop	dropped
6.	plant	planted
7.	wash	washed

8. note — noted

9. chase — chased

10. provide — provided

EXERCISE 32

1. raise — He raises
2. dress — She dresses
3. hate — He hates
4. brush — She brushes
5. fry — He fries
6. smile — She smiles
7. want — He wants
8. carry — She carries
9. push — It pushes
10. wait — He waits

1. raises — raised
2. dresses — dressed
3. hates — hated
4. brushes — brushed
5. fries — fried
6. smiles — smiled
7. wants — wanted
8. pushes — pushed
9. waits — waited
10. carries — carried

EXERCISE 33

1. waits — He waited.
2. requires — It required.
3. rushes — She rushed.
4. demands — He demanded.
5. cries — She cried.
6. screams — He screamed.
7. mates — It mated.
8. kills — He killed.
9. moves — It moved.
10. fires — He fired.

EXERCISE 34

PRESENT	PAST
1. take	took
2. run	ran
3. eat	ate
4. go	went
5. come	came
6. grow	grew
7. speak	spoke
8. fight	fought
9. hit	hit
10. fall	fell
11. fly	flew
12. swim	swam
13. tell	told

14. sing ___sang___
15. make ___made___
16. rise ___rose___
17. shine ___shone___
18. win ___won___
19. feed ___fed___
20. drink ___drank___

EXERCISE 35

1. ___writes___ wrote
2. ___wins___ won
3. ___shoots___ shot
4. ___comes___ came
5. ___goes___ went
6. ___sits___ sat
7. ___breaks___ broke
8. ___rises___ rose
9. ___swims___ swam
10. ___buys___ bought
11. ___shines___ shone
12. ___sleeps___ slept
13. ___tells___ told
14. ___lights___ lit
15. ___catches___ caught
16. ___bends___ bent
17. ___feeds___ fed
18. ___holds___ held
19. ___takes___ took
20. ___thinks___ thought

EXERCISE 36

1. Celeste (S) / is (P) a pretty girl.
2. The dog (S) / was (P) black and white.
3. I (S) / am (P) hungry for supper.
4. The men (S) / are (P) outdoors.
5. The train (S) / was (P) late tonight.
6. The stars (S) / were (P) bright in the sky.
7. This horse (S) / is (P) very smart.
8. The audience (S) / was (P) too noisy.
9. I (S) / am (P) glad to see my friend.
10. The women (S) / were (P) in the office.

EXERCISE 37

1. Richie ___is___ the best pitcher.
2. Jim and Doug ___are___ catchers on our team.
3. Julie Andrews ___was___ the star in *Mary Poppins.*
4. At night I ___am___ sleepy.
5. You think you ___are___ so smart!
6. Yesterday you ___were___ late to work.
7. Last summer Tim ___was___ working.
8. Now he ___is___ back in school.
9. This week my brother ___is___ home on leave from the army.

10. Where are you going tomorrow?

EXERCISE 38

1. She/was very mean to me.
2. They/are not nice to strangers.
3. Our family/is together on weekends.
4. We/were at the beach last Sunday.
5. The weather/was very hot.
6. It/was almost too hot to walk on the sand.
7. The waves/were very powerful.
8. Sometimes people/are not very thoughtful.
9. They/were often at home.
10. I/am pleased with your progress.

1. She
2. They
3. We
4. It
5. They
6. I

EXERCISE 39

1. I = hungry. (am)
2. He = my brother. (is)
3. The boys = members of the baseball team. (are)
4. Last year they = the high school champions. (were)
5. She = the best student in the class. (is)
6. We = very good friends. (are or were)
7. We = watching TV at my house last night. (were)
8. My mother = going out shopping. (is)
9. Last year our coach = Chuck Wilson. (was)
10. He = a very good coach all that year. (was)

EXERCISE 40

1. In the last row sits/John. Pr.
2. At the back of the room was/a huge fireplace. P.
3. Under my window grows/a beautiful rosebush. Pr.
4. On the porch in a rocking chair sat/the old, old lady. P.
5. After all the cold weather comes/the warm, lovely spring. Pr.
6. Next to my house is/a little park. Pr.
7. Down the chimney came/Santa Claus! P.
8. After the dinner came/a delicious dessert. P.
9. Inside all the tissue paper was/a tiny gold box. P.
10. Last of all, after everybody else, came/Peter! P.

EXERCISE 41

1. Next to the wall the children/planted (flowers.)
2. With great caution the robber/opened the (window.)
3. Under the trees in the shade sat/the old man.
4. With a terrible roar, the jet/passed overhead.
5. After lunch the brothers/went shopping.
6. Last of all comes/the grand prize.
7. On Saturday we/took a (trip) to Connecticut.

8. Barking angrily, the dog/charged the stranger.
9. Smiling sweetly, the lady/opened the door for the guests.
10. After the storm came/the sunshine again.

EXERCISE 42

1. The boys/caught a fish.
2. My grandmother/is Mrs. Wilson.
3. Jimmy/hit a foul ball.
4. Mary/is the oldest person here.
5. I/am your new supervisor.
6. The boy/slammed the door.
7. You/are the last one to finish.
8. Joe/carried the garbage can outside.
9. Tom/shoveled the driveway for me.
10. The students/did their work quickly.

EXERCISE 43

Follow the same directions as for Exercise 42.

1. John/is a good friend of mine.
2. He/opened the package from his sister.
3. Janet/left her purse at home.
4. That desk/is an antique.
5. We/gave a party for the couple.
6. She/is a reporter for the local newspaper.
7. They/built their house themselves.
8. Bruce/feeds his cat three times a day.
9. You/are an excellent writer.
10. I/am the best cook in my family.

EXERCISE 44

	PRESENT	PAST
1.	wash	washed
2.	fill	filled
3.	twist	twisted
4.	dress	dressed
5.	choke	choked
6.	mend	mended
7.	rain	rained
8.	land	landed
9.	mail	mailed
10.	test	tested

1. am
2. are
3. is
4. was
5. were

EXERCISE 45

PRESENT	PAST
1. I am	7. He was

2. She	is	8. I	was
3. You	are	9. We	were
4. We	are	10. She	was
5. They	are	11. You	were
6. It	is	12. They	were

EXERCISE 46

PRESENT	PAST
1. dig	dug
2. run	ran
3. sing	sang
4. think	thought
5. fly	flew
6. sit	sat
7. drink	drank
8. win	won
9. bring	brought
10. sink	sank
(Suggested Verbs)	
11. is	was
12. go	went
13. speak	spoke
14. eat	ate

EXERCISE 47

1. First we eat breakfast and then we ~~went~~ go to school.
2. Mary cut Anne's hair and curl~~s~~ed it.
3. The mother fed and change~~s~~d the baby.
4. You wash the dishes and I dr~~ied~~y them.
5. We ate and ~~drink~~ drank well.
6. The boys fight and yell~~ed~~ at each other.
7. The policeman stops his car and walk~~ed~~s over to the boys.
8. The fire engine roared down the street and ~~skids~~ skidded around the corner.
9. I went to the movies and then I ~~come~~ came home.
10. I am in a hurry but he ~~was~~ is not.

EXERCISE 48

A.
1. The three boys (S) / fished (P) all day in the river.
2. Bass, pickerel, and trout (CS) / were (P) their catch.
3. Low in the sky sank (P) / the sun (S).
4. The evening shadows (S) / crept (P) across the valley.
5. Home went (P) / the boys (S) with their catch.
6. Their supper (S) that night / was (P) delicious fresh fish.
7. Tim, Jack, and Joe (CS) / were (P) old friends.
8. They (S) often / went (P) fishing together.
9. One day they (S) / saw (P) a school of pickerel.
10. Now they (S) / watch (P) the river every day.

B. 1. A proper noun Jim, Jack, Joe

2. A common singular noun day, river, bass, pickerel, etc. etc.

3. A collective noun school

4. A verb of being were, was

5. A verb of action in the past tense fished, sank, crept, went

6. A direct object school, river

7. A compound subject Jim, Jack, and Joe

8. A pronoun They

9. A verb in the present tense watch

10. A predicate noun catch, fish, friends

	SINGULAR	PLURAL
C.	1. woman	women
	2. lady	ladies
	3. boy	boys
	4. wish	wishes
	5. gentleman	gentlemen
	6. mouse	mice
	7. house	houses
	8. goose	geese
	9. day	days
	10. knife	knives

	PRESENT	PAST
D.	1. wash	washed
	2. go	went
	3. fly	flew
	4. sing	sang
	5. think	thought
	6. am	was
	7. want	wanted
	8. creep	crept
	9. watch	watched
	10. run	ran
	11. wander	wandered
	12. ring	rang
	13. buy	bought
	14. are	were
	15. swim	swam
	16. stop	stopped
	17. is	was
	18. belong	belonged
	19. wear	wore
	20. blossom	blossomed

E.	1. I	am
	2. He, She, It	was
	3. you, we, they	were
	4. you, we, they	are
	5. He, She, it	is

F. 1. Yesterday he was here.

2. Tomorrow I am going home.

3. They were at the picnic last week.

4. She is the happiest person I know.

5. We are leaving right now.

EXERCISE 49

1. What do you want? Q
2. I want to go with you. S
3. Jim hit John. S
4. Why did he do that? Q
5. It was not John's fault. S
6. Jim has a nasty temper. S
7. Where are you going? Q
8. I am going to work. S
9. Do you like your boss? Q
10. No, he is too crabby. S

How many questions did you find? 4

EXERCISE 50

1. What shall we do now? Q
2. Shall we go fishing? Q
3. No, I don't feel like fishing. S
4. Would you like some ice cream? Q
5. This is good, isn't it? Q
6. Tomorrow is my day off. S
7. What will you do? Q
8. I hope it doesn't rain. S
9. I have to paint the house. S
10. Wouldn't you like to help me? Q

EXERCISE 51

1. Go on home now. C
2. Oh! I forgot something! E
3. Turn off the headlights. C
4. Quick! Call the police! E or C
5. Please shut the door. C
6. Don't walk on the grass. C
7. Hey! Guess what happened! E or C
8. Call me up tonight. C
9. Long live the king! E
10. Please pass in your papers. C

EXERCISE 52

1. (you) Hand me that book. C
2. Hear this. Now (you) hear this. C
3. What a wonderful idea! E
4. Gee, that would be great! E
5. Please (you) tell me what happened. C
6. It's a deep, dark secret! E
7. (you) Turn right at the corner. C
8. Holy cow, look at that! E or C
9. (you) Get a move on, you guys. C
10. (you) Get going before you get caught. C

EXERCISE 53

1. What time is it? Q

2. Drop that gun. C
3. George was late to work. S
4. Nina, come here at once. C
5. Don't you think Patty reads well? Q
6. The telephone rang for a long time. S
7. How fast the children ran! E
8. Please put it on the table. C
9. May I borrow that book? Q
10. Joe needs another pencil. S

EXERCISE 54

1. Come in, please. C
2. Why are you late? Q
3. Quick, call a doctor. C
4. That is a pretty dress. S
5. Do you like it? Q
6. I think it's lovely! E
7. It is time for lunch. S
8. Do you like to swim? Q
9. Close that window. C
10. It's a beautiful day. S

EXERCISE 55

A
1. What kind of sentence ends with a question mark? Question
2. What kind of sentence makes a statement of fact? Statement
3. What kind of sentence has an implied subject *You*? Command
4. What kind of sentence expresses excitement? Exclamation
5. What must every sentence begin with? Capital

B
1. Please pass the butter. C
2. Why are you so late? Q
3. It is much colder tonight. S
4. My goodness, what a surprise! E
5. What happened? Q
6. Somebody got hurt. S
7. Gosh, that's terrible! E
8. Did you call a doctor? Q
9. Help, call the police! E or C
10. They're already here. S

C
1. What time is it? Q
2. It is seven o'clock. S
3. Pass the bread, please. C
4. It is time for bed. S
5. Get to bed, boys. C
6. Henry broke his leg. S
7. How did he do that? Q
8. Quick, get a doctor! E or C
9. Get Dr. Fox on the telephone. C
10. He's coming right over. S

11. what are you doing ? Q
12. it's none of your business. S
13. don't get fresh with me. C
14. are you looking for trouble ? Q
15. gosh, you must be nuts! E
16. why don't you get lost ? Q
17. I have a sore throat. S
18. get out of the way . C
19. do you think you can win ? Q
20. ouch, that hurt! E

EXERCISE 56

1. ~~went down the street~~
2. two girls went down the street.
3. they waited on the corner.
4. ~~running down the path~~
5. ~~when she went in the house~~
6. ~~suddenly a voice~~
7. suddenly Nancy heard a voice.
8. ~~in the gray light of dawn~~
9. the boys went fishing.
10. ~~and ran to the window~~

How many complete sentences did you find? 4

EXERCISE 57

1. ~~three cars are~~
2. three cars are colliding.
3. ~~the cop on the corner~~
4. the cop on the corner has a gun.
5. ~~after my lunch~~
6. soon the bell rang.
7. ~~turned on the light~~
8. my mother turned on the light.
9. ~~when the doorbell rang~~
10. when the doorbell rang I opened the door.

EXERCISE 58

(Suggested Sentences)

1. when the siren sounded
   When the siren sounded I jumped.
2. rushing downstairs, Sally
   Rushing downstairs, Sally tripped.
3. Norman said that he
   Norman said that he would do his homework.
4. and sat down to watch TV
   He had a snack and sat down to watch TV.
5. on a hot summer day
   On a hot summer day you can find the family at the pool.
6. like to swim
   I like to swim.
7. John and Bill also
   John and Bill also like to play golf.

8. rang again and again
The telephone rang again and again.

9. up the ladder
He climbed up the ladder to fix the roof.

10. later in the day
The reception was held later in the day.

EXERCISE 59
(Suggested Sentences)

1. ran into the house
She picked up the kitten and ran into the house.

2. the lamp on the table
The lamp on the table is a new one.

3. my lunch at work
I always eat my lunch at work.

4. I wish I had taken
I wish I had taken my mother's advice.

5. too cold to go
It was too cold to go swimming.

6. right after breakfast
Right after breakfast I did the dishes.

7. standing quietly in the corner
The boy was found standing quietly in the corner.

8. their friends and relatives
Their friends and relatives attended the wedding.

9. before dark
Her mother said she had to be home before dark.

10. it was very
It was very generous of them to lend us the money.

EXERCISE 60

1. Y your letter came yesterday. I read it. A afterwards I showed it to my buddy.
2. H his umbrella blew away in the wind. I it went flying down the street.
3. T the cat was angry. S she started clawing me. T then I hit her.
4. M my wife asked me to go to the store. I forgot all about it.
5. S someone called my name. I turned around. T there was my friend Joe.
6. I read about him in the paper. I it said he was a great pitcher.
7. Jim wanted to go to the movies. H his girl friend wanted to go dancing.
8. A a big plane was flying over the house. S suddenly we heard an explosion. W we ran outside.
9. A all we could see was dust. T then suddenly flames sprang up.
10. P people were screaming. I tried to get close. T the flames were too hot.

EXERCISE 61

1. after the show we went to the drugstore. we each had a Coke.
2. yesterday was my mother's birthday. I forgot to buy her a present.
3. he heard a noise. it was outside his window.
4. when she left work it was raining. she took a taxi home.
5. it's too cold in here. I think I'll get my sweater.
6. my brother asked me to drive him to work. I couldn't because my car was being repaired.
7. last night we came home late. we got caught in a traffic jam.
8. I wish I had a bike. then I could ride to work.
9. she starts her new job this week. I hope she likes it.
10. maybe they will visit us soon. we enjoy their company

How many sentences did you find? 20

EXERCISE 62

A

1. What is a sentence?
   It expresses a complete thought.
2. What are the two parts of a sentence?
   Subject and Predicate
3. What must a sentence begin with?
   Capital letter
4. What must a sentence end with?
   Punctuation (or period)
5. What is a run-on sentence?
   Separate sentences strung together

B

1. where are you going, my pretty maid?
2. ~~after we go to the show~~
3. I would like a drink of water.
4. he went to work. then he came home for dinner.
5. ~~because it is so hot~~
6. first she wrote the report. after that she went to the meeting.
7. after all that, she was tired out.
8. he's a big tall guy with red hair.
9. ~~although he gets his work done~~
10. first he did setting-up exercises. then he took a hot shower.

(Suggested Sentences)

C

1. my father and I
   My father and I often go to the ball games.
2. where did you
   Where did you go when you left the house?
3. the planet Mars
   The planet Mars is the red planet.

4. oh, my goodness
Oh, my goodness, I forgot my car keys!

5. ran faster than ever
Our horse ran faster than ever at this morning's race.

6. why were they
"Why were they late?" asked the teacher.

7. the people in our car pool
The people in our car pool gave Joe a surprise birthday party.

8. out of the window
By looking out of the window, I can see the New York skyline.

9. fell flat on his face
He slipped on the pavement and fell flat on his face.

10. the teacher's dress
The teacher's dress was very stylish.

11. when did she
When did she have the baby?

12. the fellows in this block
The fellows in this block all belong to the same club.

13. ran down the street
The thief ran down the street and was caught.

14. with the siren screaming
With the siren screaming, the police car turned the corner.

15. good heavens
Good heavens, look at that!

16. what is that
What is that dance called?

17. the last thing
What is the last thing you remember?

18. did he ask
Did he ask you if he could borrow the car?

19. out the window
The canary flew out the window.

20. why in the world
Why in the world would you want to do that?

EXERCISE 63

1. The supervisor said, "Let's start our meeting."
2. Alex announced, "Our new cleaning products are very popular."
3. Mary stated, "We made a large profit from them in the first six months."
4. Susan remarked, "They sell best in the Middle West."
5. Bill replied, "That's where we have done the most advertising."
6. Mary suggested, "We need more radio ads in other parts of the country."
7. Alex said, "It's important to find out why our customers prefer our products."
8. Susan said, "Let's make a survey of our customers in the Middle West."
9. Bill answered, "That's a great idea."
10. The supervisor said, "Now we'll discuss those radio ads."

EXERCISE 64

1. Sarah announced, "I'd like to go camping for our vacation."
2. Bob said, "That's impossible because we don't have any camping equipment."
3. Sarah answered, "We could borrow the Nelsons' equipment."
4. Bob said, "OK, but we need to decide where we're going."
5. Sarah suggested, "I think Ontario would be a lovely place to camp."
6. Bob sighed, "Yes, but that would be a long drive."
7. Sarah replied, "Well, we could camp along the way."
8. Bob said, "But we have only two weeks of vacation."
9. Sarah said, "I guess that isn't enough time."
10. Bob suggested, "We could camp at one of the state parks near here."

EXERCISE 65

1. "I got a raise," announced Sally at dinner.
2. "I'm very pleased to hear it!" exclaimed her mother.
3. "You've worked very hard for that," said her father.
4. "I think this calls for a celebration," he added.
5. "I think so, too," Sally's mother said.
6. "I don't see anything so great about it," growled her brother.
7. "That's just because you're jealous," snapped back Sally.
8. "Now don't quarrel at dinner," said their mother.
9. "I was going to suggest a treat for all of us,"
10. "In that case, it's OK with me," announced Sally's brother.

EXERCISE 66

1. "I'd like to go camping for our vacation," Sarah announced.
2. Bob said, "That's impossible because we don't have any camping equipment."
3. "We could borrow the Nelsons' equipment," Sarah answered.
4. Bob said, "OK, but we need to decide where we're going."
5. Sarah suggested, "I think Ontario would be a lovely place to camp."
6. "Yes, but that would be a long drive," Bob sighed.
7. Sarah replied, "Well, we could camp along the way."
8. "But we have only two weeks of vacation," Bob said.
9. Sarah said, "I guess that isn't enough time."
10. "We could camp at one of the state parks near here," Bob suggested.

EXERCISE 67

1. "Where are you going?" asked the young woman.
2. "I'm going running," answered the young man.
3. "Can I come with you?" she asked.
4. "Of course you can!" he exclaimed.
5. "I like having company when I run," he added.
6. "Oh, and I love the exercise," said the young woman.
7. "When did you start running?" asked the young man.

8. "I started about two years ago," she said.

9. "I wanted to keep in shape," she added.

10. "Come on, let's go," he said.

EXERCISE 68

1. "Where am I?" asked the bearded man.
2. "You are in the hospital," said the nurse.
3. "The hospital! Good heavens!" exclaimed the man.
4. "Now, don't get excited," the nurse said. "We will take good care of you."
5. "What happened to me?" asked the man.
6. "You were hit by a car," said the nurse. "Don't you remember anything?"
7. "I remember riding my motorcycle," the man said. "I don't know what happened after that."
8. "Am I going to get well?" he asked.
9. "Of course you are!" exclaimed the nurse. "The doctor will soon be here."
10. "Thank goodness for that," sighed the man.

EXERCISE 69

A 1. Where on earth have you been? Q

2. Heavens, you had me worried to death! E

3. Don't you ever run off like that again. C

4. I was afraid you had been run over. S

5. Why didn't you telephone me? Q

6. I would have come and picked you up. S

7. Listen to me when I'm talking to you. C

8. You are simply impossible. S

9. You owe me an explanation. S

10. Good gracious, she's running away again! ____

B 1. "Where are you going?" asked the police officer.

2. "I'm not telling," the little boy said.

3. The police officer looked at him and asked, "What's your name?"

4. "I won't tell you," answered the boy.

5. "Does your mother know you're out?" asked the officer.

6. The little boy muttered, "No."

7. "Don't you think she'll worry?" the officer said.

8. "She won't care," said the little boy.

9. "Here comes a lady now," said the officer.

10. "Billy, where have you been?" the lady cried. "You had me worried sick."

EXERCISE 70

1. This is the first day of October.
2. Tom and Dick both live in Springfield.

3. star light, star bright,
first star I see tonight.

4. marie and ellen live in pittsburgh.

5. thank you for the book you sent me for christmas.

6. should old acquaintance be forgot and never brought to mind?
should old acquaintance be forgot and days of auld lang syne?

7. columbus discovered america on october 12, 1492.

8. rick brought katie to the party.

9. there is a zoo in central park in the middle of new york city.

10. george washington lived in mt. vernon, virginia.

EXERCISE 71

1. my birthday is on saturday, october 23.

2. joe's birthday is the next day, sunday.

3. joe and victor are my best friends.

4. the president of the united states lives in the white house.

5. roses are red, violets are blue,
sugar is sweet and so are you.

6. i love christmas even better than thanksgiving.

7. columbia university is in new york city.

8. dr. fisher is our family doctor.

9. near us is the coliseum.

10. my country, 'tis of thee,
sweet land of liberty,
of thee I sing.

EXERCISE 72

1. o give thanks unto the lord for he is good.

2. i wish i had a new ford.

3. my father reads the daily news.

4. oh nuts, i forgot my lunch!

5. why, o why, am i so stupid?

6. the wind in the willows is a good book.

7. show me thy ways, o lord; teach me thy paths.

8. have you read the adventures of tom sawyer?

9. my composition is called the first president of the united states.

10. the lord is my shepherd; i shall not want.

THE DAFFODILS

i wandered lonely as a cloud
that floats on high o'er vales and hills,
when all at once i saw a crowd,
a host of golden daffodils,
beside the lake, beneath the trees,
fluttering and dancing in the breeze.

William Wordsworth

EXERCISE 73

1. my name is joseph w wiley.
2. i live at 3 rutland rd. in great neck, n y
3. the ship is commanded by capt. peter smith.
4. the director of the f b i lives in washington, d c
5. gen. johnson commands the armed forces of the u s a
6. i got a b s degree from city college.
7. rev. keating lives at 35 w. fourteenth st, n y c
8. mr. and mrs. j. williams, jr. live at 19 lynn rd., springdale, mass.
9. samuel schulman, m d has an office in the medical bldg.
10. his office hours begin at 10 a m

EXERCISE 74

1. P. M. Afternoon (Post Meridian)
2. F. B. I. Federal Bureau of Investigation
3. B. C. Before Christ
4. A. D. Anno Domini
5. U. N. United Nations
6. P. O. Post Office
7. U. S. A. United States of America
8. N. Y. C. New York City
9. M. D. Medical Doctor
10. A. M. Morning (Ante Meridian)

EXERCISE 75

1. thomas jefferson wrote the declaration of independence.
2. george washington was our first president.
3. abraham lincoln composed the gettysburg address.
4. the battle of bunker hill began the american revolution.
5. the liberty bell is in a museum in philadelphia.
6. the empire state building used to be the tallest building in the world.
7. radio city is at 49th st. and fifth ave. in new york.
8. the mississippi river flows into the gulf of mexico.
9. hawaii and alaska are our newest states.
10. children believe santa claus lives at the north pole.

EXERCISE 76

1. Street St.
2. Road Rd.
3. January Jan.
4. December Dec.
5. Monday Mon.
6. Tuesday Tues.
7. Wednesday Wed.
8. October Oct.

9. Nebraska Neb. or NE
10. Connecticut Conn. or CT
11. Thursday Thurs.
12. February Feb.
13. Massachusetts Mass. or MA
14. Friday Fri.
15. November Nov.
16. Mountain Mt.
17. Doctor Dr.
18. Professor Prof.
19. Saturday Sat.
20. General Gen.

EXERCISE 77

A.
1. george, elvis, and john have a rock group, the weirdos.
2. thanksgiving day comes on november 22 this year.
3. dr. anderson lives in mt. hermon, mass.
4. hear me, oh lord, when i pray unto thee.
5. julie's father is in the f.b.i.
6. prof. dennis teaches at columbia university.
7. the name of my book is a tale of two cities.
8. saturday is my favorite day of the week.
9. i will send your package c.o.d. to 231 main st. springfield, mass.
10. sing a song of seasons,

something bright in all,

flowers in the summer,

fires in the fall!

B.
1. where are you going? asked my brother.
2. out to play baseball, i answered.
3. he shouted after me, hey, can i come?
4. oh i guess so, i said.
5. we headed down main street toward prospect park.
6. dr. j. j. robbins works at the dallas city hospital.
7. corp. g. steward lives at 10 main st. denver, col.
8. judy said she would be home by 12 p.m.
9. she didn't come until 2 a.m.
10. boys flying kites haul in their white-winged birds,

you can't do that way when you're flying words.

thoughts unexpressed may sometimes fall back dead,

but god himself can't change them once they're said.

Will Carlton

EXERCISE 78

1. The slim, long-haired girl / waited on a busy corner.
2. She / wore a pink shirt and ragged blue jeans.
3. My new car / has bucket seats and red upholstery.

4. The big brown dog chased the frightened thief.

5. The brightest girl on our block is little Beth.

6. The big black cat sat in the sunny window of the grocery store.

7. On cold winter nights I like a blazing fire.

8. The icy wind blows stinging snow down the narrow streets.

9. But in our cheerful kitchen is a warm stove.

10. His plump rosy mother hums an old Italian song while she cooks delicious lasagna.

EXERCISE 79

(Suggested Adjectives)

1. The young girls giggled as the handsome boys walked by.

2. A tall skyscraper is being built overlooking the picturesque bay.

3. A stiff breeze blew in from the stormy ocean.

4. He drove his red convertible down the lonely highway.

5. A large basket of flowers stood on the picnic table.

6. A young girl rode on the small bicycle.

7. The happy boy was eating vanilla ice cream with chocolate sauce.

8. In my grandmother's country house I could smell a delicious pie baking.

9. On Monday morning the woman wore a blue blouse and a checked skirt.

10. She had black shoes and a new pocketbook.

EXERCISE 80

1. My house is green.
2. The supper was delicious.
3. The boys were noisy.
4. Your picture is beautiful.
5. The weather was hot.
6. But the evenings were cool.
7. I am busy this week.
8. That school is big.
9. My boss is strict.
10. But she is fair.

EXERCISE 81

1. My house is white with green shutters.
2. My rattly old car was blue.
3. His new convertible is red with a black top.
4. The cool cotton dress is blue and white.
5. The young people were happy and noisy.

6. I/am sad and lonely tonight.
7. We/are crowded in our small apartment.
8. The park/is lovely in the warm spring weather.
9. The busy highway/is full of speeding cars.
10. The giant plane/is high over the gray storm clouds.

EXERCISE 82

1. I am taller than my brother. 2
2. My father is the tallest in the family. 3+
3. You are the nicest person I know. 3+
4. My brother is much older than I. 2
5. She has the cutest baby I ever saw! 3+
6. Selma and Judy are both pretty but Judy is prettier than Selma. 2
7. A quarter is larger than a dime. 2
8. Tokyo is the largest city in the world. 3+
9. My sister is the best lawyer in town. 3+
10. The World Trade Center is higher than the Empire State Building. 2

EXERCISE 83

1. great greater greatest
2. gentle gentler gentlest
3. high higher highest
4. lovely lovelier loveliest
5. smart smarter smartest
6. funny funnier funniest
7. blue bluer bluest
8. pale paler palest
9. tiny tinier tiniest
10. tame tamer tamest

EXERCISE 84

1. a tree
2. an apple
3. a table
4. an ocean
5. an elevator
6. a pencil
7. an automobile
8. an honor
9. a lamp
10. an Indian

EXERCISE 85

1. The apples from his farm are best.
2. She wore a little red bow in her blond hair.
3. I hope you are better today.
4. You are a bad dancer but your sister is worse.
5. The ice cream vendor pushed his little cart.
6. We had delicious beef, fried potatoes, and green beans.
7. It is a good thing you have an old uncle with that much energy.
8. The TV in the next apartment makes a terrible noise.

9. I want an honest answer to my last question.

10. An eagle is faster than most birds.

EXERCISE 86

A 1. An adjective describes a noun or a pronoun.

2. A predicate adjective modifies or describes the subject of the sentence.

3. *A* is an indefinite adjective used before words beginning with a consonant.

4. *An* is an indefinite adjective used before words beginning with a vowel or silent h.

B 1. The big black dog/followed the tall man.

2. A white fluffy kitten/sat on the front stoop.

3. My old grandmother/is deaf.

4. But she/is a marvelous cook.

5. In the pouring rain he/ran home.

6. He/had forgotten an umbrella.

7. My younger son/is now taller than I am!

8. Few people/are smarter than you are.

9. That boy/is the fastest runner on the track team.

10. My wife/knows which desserts I like.

C

ADJECTIVE	MORE	MOST
1. funny	funnier	funniest
2. good	better	best
3. red	redder	reddest
4. cute	cuter	cutest
5. bad	worse	worst
6. silly	sillier	silliest
7. much	more	most
8. fast	faster	fastest
9. lovely	lovelier	loveliest
10. wise	wiser	wisest

EXERCISE 87

ADJECTIVE	ADVERB
1. loud	loudly
2. bright	brightly
3. high	highly
4. easy	easily
5. final	finally
6. silent	silently
7. usual	usually
8. close	closely
9. happy	happily
10. real	really

EXERCISE 88

1. The carpenter/hammered (noisily.) noisy

2. The child/sang (happily.) happy

3. The old lady/spoke (quietly.) quiet

4. The priest/listened (silently.) silent

5. The woman/wept (sadly.) sad

6. The mother/smiled (tenderly.) tender

7. The baby/played (busily.) busy

8. The dog/barked (loudly.) loud

9. My teacher/talks (clearly.) clear

10. The child/rubbed his eyes (sleepily.) sleepy

EXERCISE 89

1. A man/whistled (cheerfully.) cheerful

2. The sun/shone (brightly.) bright

3. A girl/sang (softly) to herself. soft

4. The black cat/purred (contentedly.) contented

5. The radio/blared (loudly) on the porch. loud

6. The train/roared (noisily) away. noisy

7. A man/skated (rapidly) across the pond. rapid

8. The driver/shouted (angrily) at his son. angry

9. The powerful car/roared (swiftly) down the highway. swift

10. The boat/drifted (lazily) on the calm sea. lazy

EXERCISE 90

1. The thief/ran (fast.) How

2. My son (always)/gets speeding tickets. When

3. I (often)/run out of money. When

4. The police/went (away) at last. Where

5. The truck driver/ate (greedily.) How

6. Tony/does (well) at his job. How

7. My boyfriend/left (early). When

8. He/answered (quickly) when I called. How

9. I/see (better) with glasses. How

10. He/traveled (far) from home. Where

EXERCISE 91

1. The poor widow wept silently.

2. The noisy boys yell loudly.

3. The men were working quietly.

4. Slowly the moon rose in the east.

5. The stars shine brightly in the sky.

6. He leaped lightly over the rocks.

7. The man spoke sadly to his priest.

8. The doctor worked quickly to dress the cut.

9. He has been exercising regularly.

10. The mother spoke lovingly to the child.

EXERCISE 92

1. My friend spoke (softly) to me.

2. The workers laughed (merrily) at the joke.

3. You have (not) finished your work.

4. The boy crept (cautiously) up the stairs.

5. They moved (creakily) under his weight.

6. I wish you would listen (carefully) to me.

7. I felt (better) after I took the medicine.

8. He did (not) like to go (far) from home.

9. We (always) eat dinner at six o'clock.

10. I (often) leave the office (late).

EXERCISE 93

1. The thief crept silently down the hall.
2. The phone on the table rang loudly.
3. He jumped nervously at the sound.
4. She comes frequently to my house.
5. I do not always see you in church.
6. Please do not yell loudly in the house.
7. They often take trips to the beach.
8. Al never told me about that.
9. He does not talk about other people.
10. But he always listens to them.

EXERCISE 94

1. The boy studied so hard for his exam.
2. She worked very carefully at her knitting.
3. Please come in more quietly.
4. She sang so sweetly that the baby stopped crying.
5. He shouted very loudly for help.
6. She criticizes more quickly than I.
7. Jack works much harder than you do.
8. I feel very well, thank you.
9. The lady spoke most kindly to him.
10. Please do not go so far from home.

EXERCISE 95

1. John drove more carefully after his accident. (more, less)
2. Mary is more dependable than Jean, who is disorganized. (more, less)
3. She works most efficiently. (most, least)
4. Please come in less noisily. (more, less)
5. Jim spoke less rudely after I had explained things to him. (less, more)
6. She answered me most graciously. (most, least)
7. The doctor operated more efficiently with good lighting. (more, less)
8. His old car travels less rapidly than mine. (more, less)
9. She solved the problem most intelligently. (most, least)
10. She works less effectively when she is tired. (less, more)

EXERCISE 96

1. Beth always behaves herself; she is a good girl.
2. Beth always behaves herself well.
3. John learned his lesson well.
4. He got a good mark on the test.
5. A good man is sometimes called a saint.
6. Nancy did her job well.
7. That is a good book.
8. Jimmy's work in the shop is good.
9. Eddie repairs cars very well.
10. I feel very well, thank you.

EXERCISE 97

1. Theresa did ~~good~~ in school today. well
2. Why don't you behave ~~good~~? well
3. You didn't paint ~~good~~ today. well
4. He did his work ~~goodly~~. well
5. Congratulations! You spoke ~~good~~ in the meeting. well
6. You learned your lesson ~~good~~. well
7. Jim did a ~~well~~ job. good
8. Jenny served the guests ~~goodly~~. well
9. Miss Johnson told a ~~well~~ story. good
10. Ted shoots a ~~well~~ game of pool. good

EXERCISE 98

1. A very big dog/barked at me.
2. Jimmy/was always hungry.
3. May/grew terribly fat.
4. My legs/are always tired!
5. She/looked more pleased than ever.
6. The boy/grew extremely tall.
7. We/are most happy about this.
8. Ted/ran very fast up the hill.
9. The stranger/came from a most distant land.
10. Patty/was so friendly today!

EXERCISE 99

weak	weaker	weakest
patient	more patient	most patient
kind	kinder	kindest
delicious	more delicious	most delicious
tight	tighter	tightest
happy	happier	happiest
fragrant	more fragrant	most fragrant
miserable	more miserable	most miserable
pleasant	pleasanter more pleasant	pleasantest most pleasant
careful	more careful	most careful

EXERCISE 100

1. Teddy runs fast. How
2. The child cried often. When
3. The old man walked slowly. How
4. The door slammed suddenly. How
5. Her phone rang immediately. When
6. I am very hungry. To what degree
7. My grandfather got too tired. To what degree
8. The little girl is just three. To what degree
9. Every day Tim grew more lonely. To what degree
10. The children are most excited! To what degree

EXERCISE 101

1. The manager spoke in a (quiet, quietly) voice.
2. Joe answered him (polite, politely).
3. He comes (regular, regularly) to my house.
4. The bull was big and (strong, strongly).
5. Janie plays the guitar (good, well).

6. Davie ate his lunch (quick, quickly).
7. His wife made him a (quick, quickly) lunch.
8. I am a (slow, slowly) thinker.
9. I think very (slow, slowly).
10. Julie's embroidery is (beautiful, beautifully).

EXERCISE 102

1. I am going to the park.
2. I want to go, too.
3. The two of us will go.
4. We want to go to church.
5. It is too hot to work.
6. I have two sisters, too.
7. It's too much trouble to do it.
8. This is too hard to read.
9. She's too busy to talk.
10. The apple is too green to eat.

EXERCISE 103

1. There is too much noise in their room.
2. Their office is over there.
3. She is in their club, too.
4. There were twenty people on their bus.
5. Their house is too far away; we can't walk there.
6. There is something I don't understand about their behavior.
7. There are the men I told you about; they are over there.
8. I left my book on the table over there.
9. There are too many people who want their own way.
10. There is no reason for their critical attitude in this matter.

EXERCISE 104
(Suggested Sentences)

there is
There is no one home.

too much
He ate too much candy.

over there
She put the package over there

their wishes
He complied with their wishes.

there are
There are no children here.

to go there
He was not old enough to go there.

too many
They asked too many questions.

to church
The women walked to church.

went there
Some very famous people went there.

their customs
Their customs were strange to us.

too hot to work
It was much too hot to work.

their names

She forgot their names.

EXERCISE 105

A. An adjective modifies a noun or a pronoun. An adverb modifies a verb, an adjective, or another adverb. Adverbs answer the questions how, when, where, and to what degree.

B. After each of the following words, write *adj* or *adv* to indicate which each one is.

kind	adj.	handsome	adj.
gently	adv.	funny	adj.
rapid	adj.	lately	adv.
green	adj.	pretty	adj.
rapidly	adv.	often	adv.
beautiful	adj.	very	adv.
good	adj.	weak	adj.
well	adv.		

C. 1. Dulcie/walked slowly home from work.

2. She/was not very happy.

3. The boss/was terribly mean to her.

4. Her mother/called loudly from the window.

5. She/was almost late for supper.

6. She/did not feel very hungry.

7. Dulcie/was often lonely.

8. But tonight she/felt more lonely than usual.

9. Then the telephone/rang suddenly.

10. Dulcie/had a very nice surprise!

D. 1. very slowly adv.

2. so heavy adj.

3. worked hard verb

4. slept restlessly verb

5. much later adv.

6. most wonderful adj.

7. so delightfully adv.

8. too heavily adv.

9. studied well verb

10. too hard adj.

E.

rapidly	how	lovingly	how
daily	when	often	when
more	to what degree	away	where
lately	when	so	to what degree
nearby	where	sometimes	when

EXERCISE 106

1. My birthday was last Tuesday, September 9th.

2. I come from Greenfield, Mass.

3. I was born on June 30, 1962.

4. My grandmother lives at 4 Locust Lane, Springfield.

5. Do you mean Springfield, Massachusetts or Springfield, Illinois?

6. Valentine's Day is on Tuesday, February 14.

7. I'll be at the Hilton Hotel, Los Angeles, California.

8. You can reach me there until Wednesday, March 18.

9. I'll be back home on Friday night, March 20.

10. My address is 16 Ridge Road, Arlington, Virginia.

EXERCISE 107

1. Well, shall we get started?

2. Yes, it's about time we did.

3. I'm afraid, however, that we will be late.

4. Oh, no, I don't agree with you!

5. Well, we shall see who is right.

6. You may, however, be surprised by what happens!

7. No, I don't think so.

8. Well, I could be wrong, I suppose.

9. Yes, you certainly could!

10. Oh, well, we'll soon find out who's right.

EXERCISE 108

1. Joe, please close the door. C

2. I asked you, Joe, to close the door. S

3. Honey, do you like this dress on me? Q

4. Are you listening to me, Peter? Q

5. Please get some ice, Julie, and bring it out here. C

6. Sheila, would you write that letter for me? Q

7. Watch out, Jim, he'll bite you! E

8. I warned you, Phil, to keep your dog tied up. S

9. Darling, where on earth have you been? Q

10. I've been waiting for you, dear, for an hour! E

EXERCISE 109

1. Our flag is red, white, and blue.

2. Today we have fried chicken, shrimps, and spareribs.

3. My favorite sports are skating, soccer, and basketball.

4. The big, brown, hungry bear headed for the campfire.

5. Dave, Ed, and Joe took off hastily when they saw him.

6. The lady was hot, tired, and cross.

7. She had been to department stores, specialty stores, and discount stores.

8. She had been jostled, bumped, and pushed around.

9. Now all she wanted was rest, peace, and quiet.

10. Instead she found her children quarreling, crying, and fighting each other.

EXERCISE 110

1. Millie, my sister, has a new dress.

2. Elizabeth II, the Queen of England, has four children.

3. Miss Cass, I want you to meet my mother, Mrs. Salerno.

4. This is my friend, Ed Mahoney.

5. The lawyer, Mr. Williams, called us to his office.

6. Our minister, Rev. Parker, preached a fine sermon.

7. My father, Jack Grillo, is a taxi driver.

8. The captain of the baseball team, Joe Murray, is my pal.

9. The tiger, a dangerous animal, does not make a good pet.

10. Paul Tribuno, the winner of the match, made a short speech.

EXERCISE 111

1. "Jimmy, where are you?" cried the mother.

2. "Jimmy," she cried, "where are you?"

3. "Come here," called the boss.

4. The boss called, "Come here!"

5. "Where is Kent Place?" the confused driver asked.

6. "Can you tell me," asked the driver, "where Kent Place is?"

7. "Turn left at the next corner," the policeman said. "It's the first street on your right."

8. "You can't miss it," he added. "There's a mailbox on the corner."

9. "Thanks, officer," said the driver, "for helping me out."

10. "Don't mention it," he replied. "I'm glad to help."

EXERCISE 112

1. Our grandmother's birthday is next Saturday, February 23.

2. "Grandmother, how old will you be then?" asked Tony.

3. We're having a party at her home at 129 14th Street, Cleveland, Ohio.

4. My mother, Mrs. Salerno, has made a big cake.

5. My cousins Tony, Joe, Douglas, and Mike are all invited.

6. Joe, however, will not be able to come.

7. "Joe, I hope you are coming to the party," said my mother.

8. "No, I can't," said Joe. "I have to go to the dentist."

9. "Well, come afterwards," suggested Tony.

10. "Yes, I could do that," said Joe. "Thanks a lot, Tony."

EXERCISE 113

1. "Waitress, can I have the meat loaf special?" asked Eddie.

2. "It's all gone but we have stew, corned beef, and fried fish," said the waitress.

3. "Oh, nuts," said Eddie. "I just feel like having meat loaf."

4. "Well," said the waitress, "how about a hamburger?"

5. "No, I had one for lunch," said Eddie.

6. "Look waitress, does the stew have dumplings?" he asked.

7. "Yes, I think so," she answered.

8. "OK, I'll try that," said Eddie.

9. "Here you are," said the waitress. "I hope you like it."

10. "Thank you, it hits the spot," said Eddie.

EXERCISE 114

1. I handed Henry the letter.
2. She gave the baby his bottle.
3. The secretary took her boss his mail.
4. The man left the waiter a tip.
5. Joe got his son a new bike.
6. He gave him the bike for his birthday.
7. Will you please pass me some coffee?
8. The live wire gave him a bad shock.
9. Mrs. Gibbs told Mrs. Murphy the latest gossip.
10. I gave Mr. Kirby your message.

EXERCISE 115

1. Marie and Debbie/ran up the steps.
2. They/put their books on the table.
3. He/took a box from the shelf.
4. Her sister/came down the stairs
5. She/invited them into the living room.
6. They/sat down on the couch.
7. We/looked at a new book.
8. Later they/went to the movies.
9. The toys/were left on the floor.
10. She/carried the dishes to the kitchen.

EXERCISE 116

	PREPOSITION	OBJECT
	on	porch
1.	up	steps
2.	on	table
3.	from	shelf
4.	down	stairs
5.	into	room
6.	on	couch
7.	at	book
8.	to	movies
9.	on	floor
10.	to	kitchen

EXERCISE 117

(Suggested Sentences)

1. A flock of sheep

A flock of sheep grazed in the field.

2. A cap with a feather

The clown wore a cap with a feather.

3. A man in uniform

A man in uniform was stationed at each exit.

4. Materials for writing

The money was used to buy materials for writing.

5. A prince of royal blood

He was a prince of royal blood and next in line for the throne.

EXERCISE 118
(Suggested Sentences)

1. jumped off the cliff

The unhappy lovers jumped off the cliff.

2. shook with laughter

They shook with laughter during the comic's routine.

3. waited at the gate

His fans waited at the gate.

4. screamed with terror

The children screamed with terror during the horror movie.

5. woven by hand

The tapestry was very old and was woven by hand.

EXERCISE 119

1. The woman waited at the door. adv.
2. The lamb followed the farmer to the barn. adv.
3. Julie wore a sweater of pure wool. adj.
4. She ran into her house. adv.
5. Jack rode his motorbike down the hill. adv.
6. Grandma's trunk is in the attic. adv.
7. She has a heart of gold. adj.
8. Susan went through the door. adv.
9. The team played in the gym. adv.
10. The horse gallops across the meadow. adv.

EXERCISE 120

1. A boy and a girl sat on the beach. adv.
2. The girl's hair was the color of corn silk. adj.
3. The boy lay on his back. adv.
4. They both basked in the sunshine. adv.
5. The roof of my house is red. adj.
6. My evening dress is of white chiffon. adj.
7. My mother made it in the evenings. adv.
8. She cut it out after work. adv.
9. I stitched the seams on the machine. adv.
10. I got my wish for a long dress. adj.

EXERCISE 121

1. The shaggy brown dog / walked ~~slowly~~ down the road.
2. The thin stooped man with gray hair / leaned ~~heavily~~ on his cane.
3. A huge fat woman with a wide smile / waddles ~~cheerfully~~ up the steps.

4. Two little boys of eight years/raced noisily up the street.

5. The great golden sun/rose majestically in the sky.

6. A graceful boat with white sails/skims lightly over the waves.

7. The frightened cat/leaped frantically for the door.

8. A crying baby/wailed pathetically in the night.

9. Four workers from the farm/jump quickly onto the truck.

10. The big friendly coach/speaks encouragingly in the locker room.

EXERCISE 122

	PHRASE	WORD IT DESCRIBES	ADJ. OR ADV.
1.	down the road	walked	adv.
2.	with gray hair	man	adj.
3.	on his cane	leaned	adv.
4.	with wide smile	woman	adj.
5.	up the steps	waddles	adv.
6.	of 8 years	boys	adj.
7.	up the street	raced	adv.
8.	in the sky	rose	adv.
9.	with white sails	boat	adj.
10.	over the waves	skims	adv.
11.	for the door	leaped	adv.
12.	in the night	wailed	adv.
13.	from the farm	workers	adj.
14.	onto the truck	jump	adv.
15.	in the locker room	speaks	adv.

EXERCISE 123
(Suggested Phrases)

1. Mr. Blake's Mr. Blake's dog.
2. The man's The man's book.
3. The girl's The girl's shoe.
4. The girls' The girls' books.
5. The lady's The lady's slipper.
6. The ladies' The ladies' handbags.
7. The men's The men's drinks.
8. Father's Father's pipe.
9. The child's The child's friend.
10. The children's The children's toys.

EXERCISE 124

1. Peter's book lay on the teacher's desk.
2. The workers' mass meeting lasted a long time.
3. "Have you seen Joan's mother?" she asked.
4. His car's brakes were not working
5. Their cars' floodlights blinded him
6. The children's voices were too loud.
7. The union's rules have to be strict.
8. This is the club members' project to raise money.
9. Mr. Blake's house is on the hill.
10. Are the women's plans completed?

I'~~a~~m	I'm	Where'~~i~~s	Where's
You'~~a~~re	You're	I'~~woul~~d	I'd
He'~~i~~s	He's	I'~~wi~~ll	I'll
She'~~i~~s	She's	I'~~ha~~ve	I've
It'~~i~~s	It's	You'~~ha~~ve	You've
We'~~a~~re	We're	We'~~wi~~ll	We'll
They'~~a~~re	They're	What'~~i~~s	What's

Negative contractions

w~~ill~~ n'~~o~~t	won't	have n'~~o~~t	haven't
does n'~~o~~t	doesn't	should n'~~o~~t	shouldn't
do n'~~o~~t	don't	did n'~~o~~t	didn't
can ~~no~~t	can't	would n'~~o~~t	wouldn't

EXERCISE 125

1. you are ___you're___
2. do not ___don't___
3. it is ___it's___
4. were not ___weren't___
5. would not ___wouldn't___
6. can not ___can't___
7. I am ___I'm___
8. they are ___they're___
9. we are ___we're___
10. I will ___I'll___
11. should not ___shouldn't___
12. will not ___won't___
13. does not ___doesn't___
14. he is ___he's___
15. I have ___I've___
16. could not ___couldn't___
17. where is ___where's___
18. I would ___I'd___
19. we will ___we'll___
20. you have ___you've___

EXERCISE 126

1. He is not ready to go yet. ___isn't___
2. Do not you have dinner ready yet? ___Don't___
3. I am as hungry as a bear! ___I'm___
4. It was not a hard test. ___wasn't___
5. We are not going this week. ___we're___
6. I will go with you when you do go. ___I'll___
7. They would not listen to directions. ___wouldn't___
8. He does not understand English very well. ___doesn't___
9. I can not explain the lesson to him. ___can't___
10. It is a beautiful day! ___It's___

EXERCISE 127
(Suggested Sentences)

1. weren't ___They weren't here.___
2. shouldn't ___You shouldn't be here.___
3. I'll ___I'll call you later.___
4. wasn't ___He wasn't available.___
5. you're ___You're next in line.___
6. don't ___Don't do that.___
7. we're ___We're moving tomorrow.___
8. hasn't ___Hasn't he finished yet?___

9. isn't Isn't it over yet?

10. doesn't Doesn't he have any?

EXERCISE 128
(Suggested Sentences)

1. can't I can't come over now.
2. haven't Haven't you eaten yet?
3. they're They're almost through.
4. you've You've already seen it.
5. wouldn't Wouldn't you like some water?
6. you'll You'll like him.
7. I've I've got a fever.
8. he's He's going to the dance.
9. I'm I'm seventeen years old.
10. she'll She'll take the box.

EXERCISE 129

1. It's very cold.
2. It's too late now.
3. It's a beautiful day.
4. Why, it's nearly lunchtime!
5. I like it because it's funny.
6. Drink this. It's delicious!
7. Now it's time to go.
8. It's going to be such fun!
9. It's hard to spell that word.
10. It's not necessary to be rude.

EXERCISE 130

1. It's time to start the meeting.
2. The bus is behind its schedule.
3. It's going to take fifteen minutes.
4. The cat chased its tail.
5. Meat loses its flavor when it's cooked too long.
6. It's a nice house; its lawn is lovely, too.
7. The cat carried its kittens in its mouth.
8. The chair has lost one of its legs because it's so old.
9. It's going to take an hour for the train to get to its destination.
10. The dog can't find its bone because it's under the refrigerator.

EXERCISE 131

1. He crawled into the cave; he looked around.
2. The teacher glanced at the clock; it was nearly noon.
3. These boys made the first team: Joe Ferrara, Tony Rocci, Henry Koch, Ed Argento.
4. The girl looked at him; she said nothing.
5. On her grocery list were written these items: apples, milk, lettuce, cereal, steak.
6. The men shouted angrily; then the women screamed back at them.
7. The manager ordered the following supplies: pencils, pads, carbon paper, tape, stencils.
8. Don't cry, Tommy; crying won't help.
9. It was terribly hot; the streets were deserted.

10. The instruments in his band were: drums, a piano, a bass sax, an electric guitar, and an electric organ.

EXERCISE 132

1. I finished the job; however, I have not been paid.
2. I wish to order the following: four lamb chops, two packages of peas, one quart of milk, and one head of lettuce.
3. These are the books I have read this year: Robinson Crusoe, The Legend of Sleepy Hollow, David Copperfield, The Last of the Mohicans.
4. My shoes are old, scuffed, and dirty; his are brand new.
5. Why, O why, can't I ever do anything right?
6. Hear us, O Lord, when we cry unto Thee; let our prayers be answered.
7. My name is Dr. J.S. Wilson; I live at 10 Woodridge Road, Chicago, Ill.
8. These are my favorite foods: bananas, peanut butter, roast beef, string beans, and cherry pie.
9. When the light turns red you stop; when it is green you may go.
10. The days of the week are abbreviated as follows: Sun., Mon., Tues., Wed., Thurs., Fri., Sat.

EXERCISE 133
(Suggested Answers)

A. 1. After parking his car, the man walked home.
2. The boys went out to play football.
3. He raced across the tennis court.
4. Going to the window, Joan opened it.
5. Opening the door quietly, the mother tiptoed into the room.
6. The women gave a shower for Debbie.
7. The fun began when she came.
8. When all the presents were opened, the women had refreshments.
9. Then they all helped to clean up.
10. After the party Kathie and Sue left.

C. 1. Christmas Day is on Thursday, December 25.
2. Oh, I didn't know it comes so soon!
3. Well, I still have to shop for my mother, my father, and my girl friend.
4. I hope Uncle Oscar arrived safely.
5. My friend Patty has invited me to a holiday party.
6. "It's going to be such fun!" she said.
7. My supervisor, Mrs. Newton, lives at 83 Davis St., Greenville, Mass.
8. Her daughter, Carol Newton, is a good friend of mine.
9. We were both born on Aug. 22, 1962.
10. We did not know each other, however, until last year.

D. 1. "Tony, have you loaded that truck?" asked the boss.

2. The winter months are December, January and February.

3. It's so hot outside I had to come in.

4. Bless me, O Lord, and answer my prayer.

5. The letter is dated Saturday, Sept. 9, 1981.

6. My favorite meal is hamburgers, baked beans, and a glass of milk.

7. Our cat, a Siamese, has blue eyes.

8. Its fur is long, soft, and fluffy.

9. "I called and called," said the boy, "but nobody answered."

10. The boy's voice however, couldn't be heard over the radio's blasting.

E.

1. girls' team	6. baby's bottle
2. children's toys	7. doesn't drive
3. can't talk	8. sheep's wool
4. men's coats	9. haven't got
5. ladies' dresses	10. you'll go

EXERCISE 134

1. My parents love me/(but) they get angry at me.
2. Do your work well/(or) you will be fired.
3. He missed his train,/(for) his taxi was caught in heavy traffic.
4. Jim wanted a new bike/(but) he couldn't afford one.
5. The next Friday was his birthday/(so) his father bought one for him.
6. We went to the clambake/(and) Charlie ate at least ninety clams.
7. I like the meat/(but) I don't want the vegetables.
8. You must practice hard/(or) you won't do well.
9. We waited a long time,/(for) Hal was late.
10. Then the door opened/(and) he walked in.

EXERCISE 135

1. I am late. I lost my way. *because*

   I am late because I lost my way.

2. You go now. I'll come later. *and*

   You go now and I'll come later.

3. The game was over. I went home. *so*

   The game was over so I went home.

4. The bell rang. No one answered it. *but*

   The bell rang but no one answered it.

5. Mary ran to the door. She knew who was there! *for*

   Mary ran to the door for she knew who was there!

6. Mrs. Smith took the inventory. Then she ordered more supplies. *and*

Mrs. Smith took the inventory and then she ordered more supplies

7. Debbie baked a pie. They would have dessert. *so*

Debbie baked a pie so they would have dessert.

8. Get out of here. Don't come back. *and*

Get out of here and don't come back.

9. It didn't hurt at first. Later it hurt a lot. *but*

It didn't hurt at first but later it hurt a lot.

10. I couldn't do my homework. I didn't have time. *because*

I couldn't do my homework because I didn't have time.

EXERCISE 136

1. "Bah and humbug!" said Scrooge.
2. Lo, a miracle happened!
3. Oh, my! I almost forgot!
4. Nuts! I should have known better.
5. Whew! That was a narrow escape!
6. Alas, we must say farewell.
7. Hurray! We won the lottery!
8. Hey, wait for me!
9. Have mercy upon us, O Lord!
10. Ouch! I cut my finger!

EXERCISE 137

1. My goodness, I forgot my dental appointment!
2. Hey, where do you think you're going?
3. Good Lord, what's going on here?
4. Hear my prayer, O Lord, and be merciful.
5. Pow! Robert hit the crook hard.
6. Ding, dong, the bells are ringing.
7. Gee whiz, that's not fair!
8. The boy fired his toy gun, bang, and the bird flew away.
9. Boy, you made a strike!
10. We won! Hurray for our team!

EXERCISE 138

What part of speech is followed by a noun, forming a phrase? Preposition

What part of speech expresses excitement or emotion? Interjection

What part of speech joins words and groups of words in a sentence? Conjunction

1. The police (in the patrol car) / drove (down the road.)
2. Ouch! I / caught my finger (in the door!)
3. Pete and Dave / fished (in the river.)
4. The girls (on the stage) / sang and danced (before the audience.)

5. The food/was very hot, but it/was tasty.

6. The foreman/was very strict (in the factory.)

7. (On the street,) though, he/laughed and fooled (with the workers.)

8. I/took my brother (to the circus) (on his birthday.)

9. Gee, we/ate lots (of popcorn,) for it/was delicious!

10. I/liked all the animals, but the elephants/were the best (in the show.)

1. Prepositional phrases used as adjectives. in the patrol car. on the stage. of popcorn.

2. Prepositional phrases used as adverbs. down the road. in the door. in the river. before the audience. in the factory. on the street. with the boys. to the circus. on his birthday. in the show.

3. Interjections. Ouch! Gee

4. Conjunctions used in compound subjects and predicates. and and

5. Conjunctions used to join two complete sentences. but for

EXERCISE 139

1. I/love my children. verb

2. Love/is a wonderful feeling. noun

3. The children/taste the new dessert. verb

4. My sister/has good taste in clothes. noun

5. My mattress/has a broken spring. noun

6. All the flowers/bloom in the spring. noun

7. The kids/spring on the trampoline. verb

8. We/went to a dance last night. noun

9. They/dance well together. verb

10. I/would enjoy his talk if he/didn't talk so much. noun verb

EXERCISE 140

1. I played with him during the noon recess. adj.

2. My mother came home at noon. noun

3. The dog barks at the child. verb

4. His bark is worse than his bite. noun

5. The ring of the bell woke Jerry. noun.

6. Please ring for the nurse. verb.

7. My shirt is made of cotton. noun.

8. Janet wore a new cotton dress. adjective.

9. Roger put the money in his pants pocket. adjective.

10. The dog pants for water because he is hot. verb.

EXERCISE 141

A. 1. What a beautiful day! E

2. It's too nice to stay inside. S

3. Go on out and get some exercise. C

4. Don't you want to go out? Q

5. I'll help you with your homework later. S

6. What are you waiting for? Q

7. Help me carry these packages. C

8. What's the matter? Don't you feel well? Q

9. Quick, call a doctor! E

10. I knew something was wrong. S

B. 1. Peter, David, and Jeff are brothers.

2. They live at 35 Spring St., Houston, Tex.

3. Peter, the oldest, was born on Apr. 21, 1965.

4. "Jimmy, will you please come here?" called his friend.

5. "I can't now, Joe," shouted Jimmy. "I'm right in the middle of this."

6. "It's all right," said his friend. "I found what I wanted."

7. The minister, Rev. Carey, came into the room.

8. She put the camera back in its case.

9. Men's shoes and ladies' hats are on the fifth floor.

10. "Oh Lord, what am I going to do now?" she sighed.

C. 1. We went to their house for dinner. (their, there)

2. Betsy has done her work well. (good, well)

3. It's too cold to go outside. (too, to, two)

4. There are some good books here but this one is the best. (their, there; better, best)

5. Doris grows more lovely every day. (lovely, lovelier)

EXERCISE 142

1. Oh, the needles and pins / are in my workbox.

2. Mr. Baldwin, the president, / came into the office.

3. The clerks / listened very quietly to him.

4. He / lectured and scolded them.

5. A flock of geese / flew over the trees.

6. The dark leaden sky / was heavy with rain.

7. (you) Joe, please / pass the bread.

8. Jerry / is the strongest boy on the team.

9. High in the sky the sun / shone.

10. There is / Mrs. Kaufman, our neighbor.

1. A singular common noun workbox, president, office, flock, sun, neighbor, boy, team, sky, rain, bread.

2. A plural common noun needles, pins, clerks, geese, trees.

3. A proper noun Mr. Baldwin, Jerry, Mrs. Kaufman, Joe.

4. A compound subject needles and pins

5. A compound verb lectured and scolded

6. A predicate noun boy

7. A noun of address Joe

8. An appositive noun president, neighbor.

9. A collective noun flock, team

10. A verb of being, present tense are, is

11. A verb of action, past tense came, listened, lectured, scolded, flew, shone.

12. A direct object bread, them

13. A predicate adjective heavy

14. A pronoun as subject He

15. A pronoun as object them

16. A prepositional phrase modifying a noun of geese, on the team.

17. An adverb modifying a verb quietly

18. An adverb modifying another adverb very

19. An interjection Oh

20. A conjunction and

21. A prepositional phrase modifying a verb in my workbox, into the office

22. Give the present tense of *flew* fly

23. Give the present tense of *shone* shine

24. Give the "most" form of an adjective strongest

25. Give an irregular plural noun geese

EXERCISE 143

A. 1. "Pete, are you going to the baseball game?" asked Ted.

2. "Who wants to watch the Mets lose again?" said Pete.

3. "Oh, well," said Ted, "it's better than staying home watching television."

4. Tomorrow is my birthday; I was born on Tues., Aug. 31, 1955.

5. When I was small we lived in Chicago at 151 Spring St.

6. My uncle's car hasn't a spare tire.

7. Dr. Spencer came to dinner on Thanksgiving Day.

8. My boss, Mr. J. T. Morris, doesn't take any nonsense.

9. Bobby's little brothers are Jimmy, Arthur, and Dick.

10. The boys' bats and mitts lay all over the porch.

B. 1. I washed the dishes and made the beds; then I vacuumed the rug. S

2. What a lot of work you did! E

3. Did your mother thank you? Q

4. Stop making so much noise. C

5. When I was ready for school , I left (or went, or started)

C. 1. The Pope (S) / gave (P) his blessing to the crowd.

2. The dog (S) in the last kennel / barks (P) loudly.

3. The family (S) / spent (P) Labor Day at their grandmother's house.

4. Up the quiet street skipped (P) / Julie (CS) and Judy, the twins.

5. They (CS) / laughed (CP) and chattered merrily.

6. Their mother (S) / called (P) them but they (S) / skipped (P) on.

7. We (S) / are (P) the two fastest runners on the track team.

8. The boy (S) in the corner / is (P) very tall.

9. Millie (S) / wants (P) us to go with her.

10. But we (S) / are (P) much too busy.

D. 1. A proper noun Pope, Labor Day, Julie and Judy, Millie

2. A common singular noun blessing, dog, kennel, house, street

3. A collective noun crowd, family

4. A noun used as a direct object blessing, Labor Day

5. A plural pronoun used as a subject we, they

6. A pronoun used as an object them, us

7. An adverb modifying a verb loudly, merrily

8. An adjective modifying a noun last, fastest, two, quiet

9. A predicate nominative runners

10. A compound sentence (give its number) 6

11. A compound subject Julie and Judy

12. A compound verb laughed and chattered

13. A verb of being in the present tense are, is

14. A verb of action in the present tense barks, wants

15. A prepositional phrase used as an adjective in the last kennel, team, in the corner.

16. A prepositional phrase used as an adverb at their grandmother's house, up the quiet street, with her

17. A predicate adjective tall, busy

18. A noun in apposition twins

19. An adverb modifying an adjective too, very

20. A conjunction and, but

E. 1. policeman policemen

2. family families

3. leaf leaves

4. noise noises

5. mouse mice

F. 1. gave give

2. spent spend

3. was is

4. sang sing

5. chattered chatter

	Adjective	*More*	*Most*
G.	1. proud	prouder	proudest
	2. good	better	best
	3. beautiful	more beautiful	most beautiful
	4. merry	merrier	merriest
	5. bad	worse	worst

H. 1. I am

2. you are

3. He, she, it is

4. I, He, She, it was

5. You, we, they were